ONE OF THE ONE HUNDRED AND FORTY BUDDHIST TEMPLES ON THE
ISLAND OF PU-TO.

CHINA'S REAL REVOLUTION

BY
PAUL HUTCHINSON

MISSIONARY EDUCATION MOVEMENT
OF THE UNITED STATES AND CANADA
New York

COPYRIGHT,
1924, BY
MISSIONARY
EDUCATION
MOVEMENT
OF THE
UNITED STATES
AND CANADA

*Printed in the
United States
of America*

To

A. M. H.

Whose heart is in China

CONTENTS

LIST OF ILLUSTRATIONS

PREFACE

SOMETHING is happening these days in China. Any newspaper reader knows that. Talk of "revolution," or "uprising," or "disorder," is printed so continually that the West has come to think of China as in constant turmoil, although the West has little idea as to what the turmoil is all about.

There really is a revolution taking place in China. It cannot be comprehended in any account of military adventures, or in the rise and fall of politicians. It cannot be dated on any calendar. It is hard to say of it "Lo, here" and "Lo, there." But the revolution is making progress, just the same.

It is the attempt of this book to throw a bit of light upon what this revolution really is. The author knows well enough how hopeless such an attempt must be, for China is so vast, and some of the forces of change are at work so silently and so deep down in the national life that no picture can give a complete understanding. However, if by these sketches of recent movements among the students, among the women, in the homes, in the factories, and in the churches, any reader is given a faint suggestion of what China's *real* revolution is, the author's purpose will have been achieved.

My thanks must be given the *Atlantic Monthly* for permission to reprint from a previous article as part of the seventh chapter of this book. The Macmillan Company has granted the right to quote from Dr. M. T. Z. Tyau's *China Awakened*, and the Abingdon Press from Stanley High's *Revolt of Youth*. From workers of the Young Women's Christian Association I have received much material on modern conditions, especially those having to do with industry.

P. H.

CHICAGO
February
1924

I

IF MARCO POLO SHOULD COME BACK

WE stepped from the shaded quiet of the section about the British consulate into the glare and uproar of the Chinkiang waterfront. It was past ten, and already the sun, reflected from the muddied mirror of the Yangtse, was hot.

My friend shrugged his shoulders, as one who would say, "There's no help for it," and plunged into that shrieking bedlam. I followed as closely as I could, but it would have taken a better halfback than I am not to have been cut loose from his interference. I could only plow ahead through the mass of half-clad, sweating boatmen, confident that, somewhere ahead, I should catch up with Dodd.

We were making our way out a narrow pontoon that stretched between the shore and an anchored hulk at which the river steamers stopped. On both sides the junks were jammed in as thickly as the Yangtze could bear them. Some were laden, and their masters bargained off their contents to buyers on the pontoon or in other boats. Some were empty, waiting for a load, whether passengers or freight.

Scarcely had we left the shore when we were seen and our purpose deduced. Dodd had made that trip too many times before to be able to con-

[1]

ceal his objective. Immediately a shouting horde of boatmasters started toward him, intent upon renting their junks for the trip down the river.

Dodd had his favorites. Two of them were tied up now, and, fighting off the rest of the crowd as, in the famine days, the hungry had to be pushed away from the supplies in North China, Dodd dickered with the pair until he had struck a bargain with the smaller.

Instantly the clamor ceased. In an incredible silence we dropped on the deck of the little junk, her four-man crew swarmed aboard and threw off the hawser ropes, and in a few moments, having wormed our way through the encompassing craft, we were scudding downstream.

It was hot, but not so hot as we had expected. The Yangtze must be nearly a mile wide about here, and a fair breeze can generally be found in a corridor of that size. Besides, the swiftness of the current was sufficient to make some breeze of our own.

Three miles or so below us—it was impossible to judge distance accurately through the heat over that stretch of water—was the tree-covered rock that formed our goal, Silver Island. I had been tramping around with Dodd since earliest dawn, looking at temple after temple, poking down one stone-paved street after another, pausing by such a Christian holy spot as the grave of Hudson Taylor. And I was tired. My feet were tired. My eyes were tired. My mind was tired. I was perfectly willing to believe that there were a thousand Buddhist temples and ten thousand Buddhist priests in and about Chinkiang without carrying my personal survey any further.

"Can't we get out of all this?" I asked Dodd. I might have gone on to tell him that I thought his the dirtiest, hottest, dreariest city I had seen, but some lingering remnant of sense restrained me. For a missionary will contend for the fair name of "his" town if it is the veriest scum-hole. I didn't tell Dodd what I thought of Chinkiang; I just asked him if there wasn't some way of getting out of it. And he suggested Silver Island.

"There's an island a few miles down the river," he told me. "Covered with trees and temples and all that sort of thing. You'll find more priests there. But they're a better sort than these grafters who stick about the city. It's a monastery, you know, and the chaps there are really seeking peace. It's quiet, and it's generally cool. And we can stay there until evening and then have our junk dragged back up after sunset. Want to try it?"

Did I? Even that milling mob at the river bank, had I known it lay between me and a cool spot on the river, would hardly have deterred me. And I did not know.

Larger and larger grew the island as our junk drew near. At first it had seemed just a mass of green. Then the outline of temples and shrines could be seen, hidden among the trees and rocks.

[3]

Once or twice the glint of a gilded character on a lacquered shrine inscription shone out. The dull gray robe of a priest passed from the shadow through a bit of sunshine, and disappeared again.

Suddenly the water swarmed about the low rail, and our crew dashed madly from one part of the deck to another, shouting unintelligibly. Only the helmsman remained calm as we were caught in the swirling eddies formed where the mighty river smashed and sucked at the defiant rock-island. Apparently we were being driven straight upon this unyielding wall, when, at the last moment, to the triumphant shouts of the boatmen, a current swept us around a corner and alongside a pier, where lay brothers quickly made us fast.

And then peace came down upon us as though we had been suddenly wrapped in some magic mantle. There was a great banyan tree rooting out through the flagstones of the jetty casting its coolness over us and the water all about us. Back of the tree was a wide doorway, with a plant-lined courtyard beyond. Beyond that another tree, and beyond that the dark restfulness of one of the monastery buildings.

There is little formality about entering such a home of quiet. One or two of the monks come forward with a conventional word of greeting. Perhaps they speak the mystic "*O mi to fu*" that is more frequently upon their lips than any other phrase. You have only to reply with a courteous sentence or

[4]

so, and before you know it, you will find yourselves in a guest room with the inevitable tea before you.

Hot tea is, I think, the most cooling drink on earth. Take it in a cup without handles; a cup that has a cover to make sure that none of the virtue escapes. Be sure that it is real China tea, a pale yellow, with perhaps a bit of jasmine floating about to add to the flavor. Never pollute it with sugar or, what is worse, cream. Step from the glare of the Oriental sun into the shade of some roadside inn or temple. Drink it fearlessly, knowing that no germ could endure in its scalding depths. New life will come flooding into you, and you will have discovered, as the Chinese did millenniums ago, the perfect drink.

Foreign visitors did not come every day to the Silver Island monastery. It was not long before the abbot himself had been brought to sit with us. I found it hard to believe, despite Dodd's assurances, that this youngerly, cultivated, spare man could be at the head of the extensive establishment. My mental picture of an abbot had been far different.

The abbot, it developed, had been well educated. For a time he had been in politics. But the seamy side of public life, with the upset conditions of the country, had disheartened him, and he had sought in this monastery soul-satisfaction through days of inner contemplation. I gathered that his personal powers had brought him rapidly to his position.

We talked about the war. The world struggle

was entering its last stages, and the abbot, for all his retirement, had been reading and thinking about this convulsion that was being felt even on the farther rim of Asia. In a way that bore not a trace of irony or enmity he asked how we reconciled our religion with what the Christian nations were doing. He knew enough of "the Jesus doctrine" to feel that there was something wrong somewhere. I fear our answers gave him little light.

"It must be with nations as it is with men," the abbot commented, after long moments of silence. "All are bound on the wheel of desire."

After lunch—a silent, abstemious, vegetarian meal —the abbot again sought us out.

"Would you like to see some of our treasures?" he asked.

Now Dodd had already told me a few things about the treasures of the monastery, and I was eager to see them with my own eyes. What they were I cannot now in detail recall. Some of them were for ritualistic purposes. More were just things of beauty. All had been presented by those who felt they had some favor to repay. I remember one belt, all of jade, the gift of an emperor who must have been almost a contemporary of Charlemagne. Safe in the middle of the river, the priests had for centuries kept these things from the looting that has despoiled so much of the country.

"All these gifts must be very old," I ventured.

"Not all of them," the abbot replied. "Some of

[6]

GOLDEN ISLAND TEMPLE ON THE YANGTZE.

TO LAND IN THE ORIENT FROM A PALATIAL OCEAN LINER MEANS FOR MANY MISSIONARIES THE FIRST STEP INTO THE INTERIOR, WHERE, IN THE YEARS TO COME, THEY MUST JOURNEY FOR DAYS AND WEEKS AT A TIME ON AN ANCIENT HOUSEBOAT.

them are truly ancient. And most of them have
been here at least since the time of Marco Polo."

"Marco Polo! Was he here?"

"Oh, yes; have you not read his voyages?"

I had, after a fashion. But the names used by
the Venetian traveler in the thirteenth century had
been so different from those used today that I had
never obtained any clear idea as to the places Polo
visited.

"It is easy to distinguish Chinkiang," objected the
abbot. "Marco Polo tells us of Kayn-gui, at the
place where the Grand Canal crosses the great river.
Where can that be but Chinkiang?

"And do you not remember the way in which he
speaks of the temple?" the abbot persisted.

I had to admit that I did not, whereupon he began to quote a passage that was evidently as familiar
to him as one of the Sutras:

"In the midst of the river, opposite the city of
Kayn-gui, there is an island entirely of rock, upon
which are built a grand temple and monastery, where
two hundred monks, as they may be termed, reside
and perform service to the idols; and this is the
supreme head of many other temples and monasteries."

"Was it this temple that Marco Polo referred
to?" I asked.

"Probably not," the abbot answered. "Marco
Polo was here. That we know. But you see he
speaks of this temple as being opposite the city, not

several miles below it. I think he must have meant the Golden Island temple."

"But the Golden Island temple is not on an island," I objected.

"So you have been there, have you? True, the Golden Island temple is not on an island, now. But it was when Marco Polo saw it. The great river has carried in so much silt in these centuries that now it is fastened to the rest of the country."

"Time brings its changes, even in China, doesn't it?"

The abbot's eyes twinkled. He would not utter Buddhist heresy, even to a foreigner.

"It may seem so, outside the temple," he answered. "But within, all is the same."

It was true. I had been at Golden Island temple. Still the two hundred priests, or even more. Still the gilded gods, towering through the gloom of the windowless room. Still the rise and fall of the chants; the boom of the drum; the note of the bell. Still the incense. Still the prostrations. Still, in the court without, the awed faces of curious children. "All is the same."

In a little while I wandered off alone among the trees, past innumerable shrines, pausing now and then to try to decipher the inscriptions cut in the rocks, and climbing gradually, until I came out on the very top. Off to the west, on the southern bank of the river, lay the city. At one edge the pagoda that crowns the Golden Island temple stood blackly against the raw sunlight. At the other edge I could see the roofs of a mission hospital, standing atop a hill that I knew was pock-marked with graves. And the hospital, I knew, was vacant.

Sitting in the shade, I found it hard to focus my eyes on that city that I knew was sweltering in the dazzling sunshine. It proved easier to lie down and to think of the city as it must have been when Marco Polo saw it.

Marco Polo! What a liar they had thought him, when he came back to Venice to tell of cities such as Europe did not dream, of silks and merchandise so rare that few princes could aspire to their possession, and of a monarch so powerful that Europe's proudest king would appear a beggar in his presence.

"The Great Khan," Polo had declared, "may be called a perfect alchemist, for he makes his own money. He orders the people to collect the bark of a certain tree, whose leaves are eaten by the worms that spin silk. The thin rind between the bark and the interior wood is taken, and from it cards are formed like those of paper, all black. All these cards are stamped with the Khan's seal, and so many are fabricated that they would buy all the treasuries in the world. All the nations under his sway receive and pay this money for their merchandise, gold, silver, precious stones, and whatever they transport, buy, or sell. In this manner the great sire possesses all the gold, silver, pearls, and precious stones in his dominions. This is the reason why the Khan has more treasure than any other lord in the world, nay, all the princes in the world together have not an equal amount."

Of course, a man who would talk like that to Venice, Venice of the thirteenth century, must be a liar. But he wasn't. To be sure, he may have embroidered the strict truth here and there a bit, as exclusive observers of other wonders in our own time have been suspected of doing. But the essential facts were as Polo reported them. The cities were really in existence; the wealth of Cathay was no myth; the power of the Mongol emperors was very nearly equal to that of all the other rulers in the world.

Traveling in Marco Polo's day was the real thing in the way of adventure. Three and a half years from Venice to Peking! How things have changed! Fifteen days is long enough to cross the Pacific now, and it's only a couple of days from Peking to Shanghai, if the bandits don't interfere with the train schedule. Marco Polo would rub his eyes if he could come back to his beloved Cathay.

And yet, would he? Have things changed so much after all? So I thought as I lay there day-dreaming atop that island in the Yangtze that afternoon. Suppose, for instance, that Polo should come back to Hangchow, that city over which for several years he ruled as the representative of the Mongol emperor. Would it seem very different to him?

Polo wrote of it as "a very noble city named

[10]

Kinsai, which means in our language the city of heaven. And I will tell you about its nobleness, for without doubt it is the finest city in the world." Well, New York and London and Paris and Buenos Aires and some others might challenge that now. But the Chinese still speak of Hangchow as a heavenly city; they are still ready, after they have seen it, to die.

Undoubtedly, Marco, should he return just now, would find Hangchow a bit down at the heel. It is certainly not "one hundred miles in circumference," as he said it was, and he could never locate to-day his "twelve thousand stone bridges." But the rest of the picture would be much the same.

There would still be the beauties of the lake and temples and monasteries, beauties such as are to be found in few other spots. There would still be the shops with their exquisite craftmanship. There would still be the honest, lustrous silks, making up into the richest of garments. There would still be the pagodas, silent sentinels of the spirits of wind and water.

As Polo wandered by the river, the junks would look unchanged, with their high after-decks and their square-rigged sails. In the spring he would see the farmers planting their rice in the same sort of flooded paddy fields, while in other fields the water buffalo would still be lumbering along waist deep, dragging the unwieldy plow through the muck behind him.

[11]

The same canals would wander about, carrying most of the heavy traffic. Here and there along the banks the same sort of mulberry trees would rear their twisted branches. Along the narrow footpaths the coolies would still be pushing their wheelbarrows, and the agonized shriek of the axles would protest that not a drop of oil had been used upon them in all the seven intervening centuries.

When the day grew hot, the traveler would step into the same sort of little inns he knew before. Here he would still have to pick his way through wheelbarrows, sedan chairs, bundles, benches, babies, loafers, dogs, other animals, and a patron or so, until he found a table that suited him, where he would sit to drink his tea. It would all be familiar.

The temples, too, would not have changed much. Some of them would have a run-down appearance. Especially would this be true of the Taoist shrines. The Confucian temples might be employed as barracks; here and there a Buddhist temple would be without its attendant. Some of the Buddhist temples would, however, look very spic and span. Great timbers imported from a state he had never heard of, called Oregon, would be seen, bearing aloft roofs that had begun to sag. But, on the whole, there would be little change. The general design would be the same, the outer courts with their hideous idol guardians of the portal, and the inner sanctuary with the deities in whose especial honor the temple existed.

[12]

Marco Polo might be surprised if he chanced upon that temple in Hangchow that contains what purports to be an image of himself, now properly exalted to the level of an "enlightened one." But he should recognize in that only the same tendency to make obeisance before any possible source of spiritual help that marked his own career.

"The Christians worship Christ; the Saracens, Mohammed; the Jews, Moses; the idolaters, Sogomombar Khan," Polo wrote. "I honor and respect all the four, and seek aid from them, as any one of them may really be supreme in heaven." One wonders if the Venetian, having noticed the readiness of the Chinese to consult any priest that offers, picked up his religious eclecticism in China.

But while much of the daily life of the country —the buying and selling, the marrying and burying, the planting and reaping—would remain almost the same, Polo would find plenty of other changes to challenge his attention.

Were he traveling from Peking to Hangchow to-day he might make the journey in de luxe trains and river steamers. Not far away from the great pagoda of Hangchow he would find a Christian college, and in its halls the Chinese student of the present would not be howling out the precepts of the ancients, but would be tracing down chemical formulæ and studying political economy.

Marco Polo would find no king in Hangchow now, nor any viceroy in the chair of state he once filled. Instead, he would see a five-barred flag, and would be told of an attempt to build a *Chung Hwa Ming Kuo*, a "Middle Flowery People's Country." This idea he would find so deeply rooted that even the disorders of a decade of rather more or less bungling attempts at democratic government had not dislodged it.

The old city wall might still stand, but it would be a very different city within the wall. And if he left Hangchow, in many places, notably the port cities, he would find the walls demolished and buildings torn down in order that broad boulevards might displace tortuous alleys. The new streets would be straight, despising the ancient superstition that had caused the mazes in which evil spirits were sure to lose themselves. Here and there a building would rise three and four stories high. Some of these would house department stores—shops on a scale to have impressed even the Great Khan. Once in a while the Venetian might even see a grandsire with his ears in a headpiece, listening in on the broadcasting from Shanghai!

The clatter of the hand-loom would still sound in many streets, but there would also be great brick and concrete buildings, out of which would come the thunder of the power looms, driven day and night. The wheelbarrow would have given place to the pneumatic-tired ricksha, and the ricksha, in turn, would see its supremacy passing as the broader streets brought in the automobile.

[14]

There would be daily newspapers and moving picture theaters, playgrounds and athletic fields, hospitals and street dispensaries, patent medicine advertisements and offers of painless dentistry, here and there a Christian church or a philanthropic institution of some kind, the Christian Associations for young men and young women, electric light plants, cigarette stores, lottery agencies, labor union headquarters; in short, such a conglomeration of unaccustomed elements as would make Marco Polo wonder whether, after all, he had come back to the same country he left so long ago.

I think that it would frighten Polo a little bit if he were to return to China today. For he knew the country intimately enough to understand what some of the problems are when a land of this size starts changing. But, after he had been in China a few months, I am sure that he would take heart. For he would find that these changes are not all on the surface. He would find them deep down at the heart of China's life. And, finding them there, he would be wise enough to see in them their promise of ultimate salvation.

All these and a lot of other ideas ran through my head that summer afternoon as I drowsed there on the island-top, looking off occasionally toward the city where Polo himself had walked so many centuries before. And even after the shadows had grown long and cool across the grass, and Dodd and I had said our farewells, and the boatmen had commenced their gallant battle homeward against the current, the notion of the change that Marco Polo would find, were he to return, did not leave me. It has not left me yet, as this will prove.

It is about this change that I write. Some people speak of it as a "revolution." It is a revolution, but there have gathered about that word connotations that make us think of battles, frenzied uprisings, overthrown governments, and like political explosions. There have been some political explosions in China in the past few years. There will be some more. But it is not with these that we are now primarily concerned. We think of China's *real* revolution, and that is something that is taking place far below the political surface of her life.

Let anything happen that concerns China's political revolution, and the newspapers of the world will print more or less accurate accounts tomorrow. But frequently the newspapers miss the changes that mark this deeper revolution that is a thousand times more important. And it is the person who does not know about this deeper revolution who loses confidence in China's future.

China has a great future. She will play her part manfully in the brotherhood of peoples. And she will do so because, even in this hour of confusion, at the center of her life, there are preparing changes that will fit her for a new day.

II

SAVED BY ITS STUDENTS

SUPPOSE you had been chief of police in Peking about the end of May, 1919. How many times a day would you have written your resignation?

Ordinarily, a job as chief of police is not to be despised. Not only are there power and prestige and a good salary attached to the office, but frequently there are many of those shadowy things known as "perquisites" that outweigh all the rest in value. That is as true in Peking as in Paris or Portland or Pittsburgh.

But being chief of police in Peking in May, 1919, was something else again. And, if the truth must be told, never since that day has the office fully regained its old glamour. It isn't an honor any more; it's a hardship. It has been ever since the days of the First Student Strike.

The chief of police was sitting in his office that May morning, a slightly puzzled frown lightly marking his ordinarily impassive features. He had been going through a trying month. News of the decision of the Paris Peace Conference to award the old German colony of Kiaochow to Japan had sent thousands of Chinese students off into a perfect frenzy of protest. And if reports were to be believed, it looked as though the students in Peking were the most frenzied of the lot!

[17]

It hadn't been so bad at the start, just fifteen thousand students marching about the streets displaying banners of protest. Nobody would have paid much attention to that. But when they stormed the home of a cabinet minister; when they wrecked his reception rooms looking for that official; when they manhandled the minister to Tokyo found hiding there—that was another matter. What was a policeman to do then but to lock up as many of the rioters as possible?

Then why all the uproar? Nothing had been proposed save a salutary admonishment, by means of the bamboo, to the thirty students captured. Why did that call for this strike? Why were all the schools still closed? At the very least, why hadn't the students gone back to their classes when their fellows were released without having been punished?

Yet they had not. They had not only stayed on strike—encouraged, the chief suspected, by their teachers—but they had made infernal nuisances of themselves by planting boxes every fifty yards or so along the streets and haranguing all who would listen on the perils of the country. If that sort of thing kept up, no one could tell what crazy ideas might be planted in the heads of the illiterate crowds, with results disastrous to all hands.

Evidently the cabinet had felt the same way about it. At least, they had ordered that such demonstrations be brought to an end. A thousand marching students had been arrested two days ago in obedience to this order. One would have thought that sufficient to have put a quietus on all this uproar. But instead, it had been necessary to arrest another thousand on the day following.

If ever a "feller needed a friend," that Peking police chief did. People, even in his own home, were beginning to look askance at him. Lads who seemed to him simply irresponsible young upstarts were being extolled in the newspapers as patriots. What was worse, his jails couldn't hold all this crowd, and his commissary wasn't ready to care for any such increased number of steady boarders. He hoped by all his ancestors that there would be no more arrests today.

A knock at the door. A subordinate, smartly saluting, and barking out his report in that expressionless staccato characteristic of every army and police force in the world: "A delegation of students to see your excellency."

"I don't want to see them."

"They say that they will wait until you leave, if necessary."

"I'll go out the back way."

"Headquarters is surrounded on all sides."

"On all sides! How big is this delegation?"

"Probably thirty thousand students."

"Thirty thousand? What are you saying? Why, that is every student in Peking!"

"Sir, they are all here!"

After that, what could the chief do but go out?

And, once he was out, and saw that mob of students, filling the courtyards and flowing away down the street in a mass that reached from wall to wall, is it to be wondered that he adopted a conciliatory tone?

"Is there anything I can do for you?" he asked the little group that stood forward as leaders.

"Lock us up!"

"Lock you up! What for?"

"For loving our country. For doing the same things that our two thousand fellow-students now in prison have done, working to protect our country from her enemies. If they are guilty, so are we. Lock us up!"

And then the police chief surrendered. Begging for a moment's respite, he withdrew into his private office, called certain chiefs of government to the telephone, explained how impossible it would be to care for another thirty thousand prisoners, told of the logical demands of the students, and asked what was to be done. In a few minutes more he returned to the waiting students to announce the release of their fellows.

Four days later the cabinet members who had been branded by the students as "traitors" resigned. A new cabinet, supposedly more loyal to the interests of China, assumed power. The students went back to their classes. Shops that had closed as a sign of sympathy for their agitation reopened. The First

Student Strike was at an end. It had shaken China, the unshakable, in exactly forty days!

What did it all mean?

Most of the newspapers that reported it saw it only as a strange political adventure on the part of a lot of adolescent boys and girls. They told of the soap boxes, and the violent speeches that were made from them. They translated the banners, and recounted the way in which unbalanced youths had bitten off the ends of their fingers in order that their sentiments of patriotism might be written in blood. They described the noisy assurance with which youngsters in their teens had withstood their elders, the officials of the nation. And when the good people of America and England and other countries of the West read those reports they were likely to remark, "If our schoolboys ever tried anything like that, we'd take them out and spank them. That's the way to deal with a situation of that kind."

But sometimes the newspapers, intent upon the surface sensation, do not catch the real significance of events. They did not during those early summer days in 1919 when the Student Movement first made itself felt in China. For that was not just a sample of unaccountable hysteria upon the part of unbalanced youth. Thinking Chinese saw in it something far more important. They saw the reassertion of the ancient supremacy of the Chinese scholar!

Was there ever another country like China in its

scale of social values? Perhaps Greece, in her Golden Age, came nearest to the same reverence for learning. But Greece was only a mite of a state, and she could not maintain her ideals long. China is a giant, sprawling across a quarter of Asia, and she held her ideals for thousands of years.

There has been no hereditary nobility in China, barring the immediate family of the emperor. (The Manchus, as foreigners, stood outside the Chinese social order.) The scholar was the truly noble man, standing at the apex of society, no matter whether he had been born in the most obscure village in the most outlying province, and had but a single coat to his back. If he had scaled the highest scholastic rank, he might enter the presence of the emperor.

And if you say that there was an exception to this, a family in which ducal rank descended from father to son, then you must see that the very exception strengthens the case. For the family thus honored was that of China's greatest sage, Confucius, the merit of whose wisdom was sufficient to carry down to his descendants throughout "ten thousand ages."

It seems to me that when we ask why China has been able to endure while all the other great civilizations have fallen, we must for much of the answer come back to this explanation. Think of a civilization—for China is as much a civilization as a nation—in which the scholar stands at the top, because the educated man is acknowledged to be the most important element in the state; with the farmer

A POLITICAL DEMONSTRATION IN WHICH THREE THOUSAND STUDENTS ENGAGED.

THE MIND TO "PROVE ALL THINGS" DEVELOPS THROUGH LABORATORY WORK IN THE ORIENT AS WELL AS IN THE OCCIDENT.

second, because he feeds men; with the artisan third, because he houses them; with the trader fourth, because he carries on business, but below the others because of his temptations to buy for too little and sell for too much; and with the soldier at the very bottom, because he is a destroyer. Could a social order like that fail to endure? Within it there may be the greater part of the contribution that China is to make to a unified world.

To be sure, the theory and the practice have not always been the same. There have been "strong men," such as the Emperor Shih Hwang-ti, who started the building of the Great Wall, who have had no use for scholars and have tried to reverse such a mollycoddle conception of society. But never with any permanent success. "In a hundred years it will all be the same," the familiar Chinese proverb has said. And at the end of the hundred years, sure enough, the scholar has assumed his sway once more.

Within the last century or so, however, the system has gradually been crumbling. Bribery undermined the honesty of the examinations in which those scholars were selected who were fit for preferment. "Pull" worked as banefully in the competitions within the ancient examination halls as it sometimes has in civil service tests in other countries. And when China was forced to deal with new types of national problems, because of the pushing in of the West, proficiency in expounding the "Eight-Legged Essay" and others of the classics written by sages

[23]

who lived millenniums ago, did not always prove a guarantee of administrative ability.

It seems ridiculous to us, this old Chinese method of securing officials. Think of cooping a young man up in a little brick stall for three days, without room to lie down, with but a candle, a brush, ink and paper, and then, if he proved able to write as Confucius or Mencius or some other worthy wrote in the long ago, sending him out to a career that might make him minister of the navy, or put him in control of the country's mines!

And yet, ridiculous as such a method was, it had its good results to show. Teachers in Western schools have sometimes said, in defending certain studies, that they had little value when it came to landing a job, but that the "mental discipline" involved made a contribution that would be of value all through life. So it must have been with the Chinese. There seems little connection between understanding the "Eight-Legged Essay" and dealing with the problems of railway construction, but the mental discipline sometimes produced minds bright enough to grapple with almost any question. At the worst, the system was hardly more ridiculous than some that have been used by Westerners in the choice of their public servants. Think of requiring of a candidate for president that he should be one who never in his life had shown enough independence to scratch a straight party ticket!

With the advent of the West in China, early in

the last century, the old order began to pass. The scholar still maintained his position, but there began to arise men who said that the test of scholarship must be very different from what it had been. Little by little they found place in the old, old language for a strange, new word, "science." It was seen that while the Westerner was undoubtedly a barbarian, knowing little of the social graces, yet he still had possessed himself of a number of things that enabled him to live in considerably more ease than the Chinese. And, after Hongkong had been cut off from China, and Tsingtau, and Indo-China, and Port Arthur, and the foreigner's railways and steamship lines had begun to penetrate the country, carrying the foreigner's goods to the farthest border, it was admitted that a new type of mind was needed to cope with this aggressive invader.

Out of this discovery came the schools based on Western models; the flight of students overseas; the new system of national education. There were times, as in the bloody summer of 1900, when the Boxer madness was upon the land, when the Chinese were ready to curse the Westerner and all his works. And there were other times when they saw in this new type of education the way to a China that should surpass in glory even the empire of the past.

The political revolution of 1911 really ushered in another period when the scholar lost his supremacy. To be sure, it was the new ideas that brought about that overturning of the Manchu throne. But when the struggle was won, and the country turned to the constructive work of building the republic that had been proclaimed, the Chinese largely forgot the student and relied upon the soldier.

Perhaps we should not blame China too much for this choice. Her contact with the West had shown her the way in which military power is able to exact its wishes. Just across the Yellow Sea she had watched an island neighbor climb from obscurity to a place among the world powers on the foundation of a first-class army and navy. And all the rush and roar of this intensely competitive life into which she had been, willy-nilly, dragged seemed to call for the "iron-and-blood heart and spirit" more than the scholar's contemplation.

In the place of the deposed boy emperor China put a typical "strong man," Yuan Shih-kai. He had achieved power as the builder of the first Chinese army according to Western models. From the ranks of his soldiers he largely drew his subordinates, and when Yuan died, these militaristic pupils of his continued in command of armies scattered throughout every one of China's eighteen provinces.

We have no space here for a discussion of the part that these *tuchuns*, or military governors, have played in the recent history of China. Theirs have been the names filling the newspapers. For the most part, they have been ignorant, brutal, selfish men, conducting their armies as their own private freebooting bands, and "living off the land" in a way that has made millions of Chinese curse the very name of soldier. When one of these generals has accumulated too much power, others have combined to pull him down. These battles have added spice to every recent summer. And because they have been interested only in the lining of their own purses and the exercise of their own despotic powers, these *tuchuns* have made anything like decent or democratic government a myth throughout the land. This has been true in every part of the country save the one or two provinces that have practically asserted their autonomy and have set up local and almost independent administrations.

Under the rule of the military men the disintegration of China has proceeded with alarming rapidity. And why not? Suppose you are offered a post in the government. Because it is you, let us suppose it to be a high post, such as a membership in a cabinet. Suppose you become minister of communications, with the development of all the natural resources—the mines, the forests, the water-power—and the building of all the railways under your control. Could you want a better opportunity to serve your country?

But you go to the capital. You find no money with which to run your department. Your salary will not pay your living expenses, for there are hordes of people, in your family and in your ministry, dependent upon you. Nobody in the cabinet dares make a move contrary to the wishes of the particular militarist whose army at the moment controls the city. And that individual is engaged with but one interest. In language that has been heard in other lands, he is "getting his while the getting is good."

One day the general sends for you. There is a foreign concession hunter who wants the control of a certain mine. Will you kindly sign the necessary papers? There will be a large portion of "graft" in it for you if you do. What if the price is ridiculously low? What if it is the general who will profit, and not the people? If you don't sign, you will be punished. Why not take your share of the universal graft?

To the honor of many a Chinese be it said that, confronted by such conditions, scores of them have resigned rather than continue in office. But, up to that summer of 1919 with which our story started, this had not seriously hampered the militarists. Other men were put in their places who were willing to sign anything for sufficient compensation. By the summer of 1919 it was reported that seventy-four per cent of all the mines in China, both developed and undeveloped, which should have brought wealth to China's own people for centuries, had been mortgaged to foreign concerns for preposterously inadequate sums. And no one could tell into whose pockets the money had gone.

It was a dismal enough outcome to less than a decade of rule by the militarist. The attempt to reverse the natural Chinese social order, a procedure said by many Westerners to hold out the only hope for a strong state, had brought nothing but disaster.

Perhaps we should not blame the militarist and his tools too heavily. Perhaps we should see that if he was willing to squander the national birthright, there were others who were eager to have him do so. In the West, during the years when China was first being opened to Occidental influences, there grew up the theory that governments should support their citizens in whatever commercial adventures they became engaged in foreign lands, without much regard to the feeling of the peoples of those lands. And so it has been that when a Western syndicate has been able to show a paper assigning to it the power to take the natural wealth of some part of China, even though that paper might be signed by a man who never held any real authority, and had been repudiated the week after he signed, Western governments have had a way of saying, "This constitutes a valid claim upon the part of our nationals, and we will back up that claim with all our forces." Western governmental support for cheap commercial intrigue of that sort has a lot to do with the present difficulties of China.

And then there has been the influence of Japan. This has to be taken into consideration, for if you ask Chinese what the cause of their country's present trouble is, a great majority of them will say, "Japan." The simple fact is that Japan sees that the basis of modern industry is iron and coal, and perhaps in the future oil. Having little of any of these indispensables, Japan has gone about trying to obtain them. Seeing them in abundance in the land of her neighbor on the Asiatic mainland, and fearing lest they might fall into other hands, she tried, for a while, to possess them by the most obvious course—diplomatic pressure, backed by military threats. But what happened in the summer of 1919, and what has happened since, has done much to convince Japan that there are better ways of securing raw materials. The power of the militarist is passing in Japan, just as it is bound to pass in China. The two countries will one day work out a commercial understanding upon a basis that will be beneficial to both of them.

But we must not get away from the early summer of 1919. Here is China, with the scholar eight years or more in the discard, and nothing to show for it but a land looted and reduced to the verge of anarchy. Over in Paris there is in session an international conference to establish world peace. China has gone to that conference seeking redress for all sorts of wrongs at the hands of the other nations. The memorandum presented by her delegates has been pronounced one of the most remarkable and irrefutable pleas for international justice ever drawn up. And it has come to pass that the issue has become symbolized in the fate of the former German territory of Kiaochow, with the railway and mines that stretch back from it across the province of Shantung.

To the Chinese the Shantung question seemed simple enough. The territory had been leased to Germany in the first place under military pressure. Japan had declared, at the outbreak of the war, that she would regain it for its rightful owners. But, once in, she showed slight intention of leaving, and had even greatly increased her holdings beyond those that the Germans had occupied. China had finally entered the war upon the same side as Japan. Surely, justice demanded that she receive back her own.

The Peace Conference decided otherwise. It was the third day of May, 1919, when the news reached China. The next day the Student Strike was afoot. It turned against the men who had been conspicuous in the sale of natural rights to Japanese, and against the Japanese themselves. The shopkeepers were induced to join forces with the students, and business came to a standstill. Within forty days, as we have seen, the first part of the student program had been achieved. The government that included the officials the students called traitors had fallen.

It took longer to carry the second phase of this program into effect. But the results were even more far-reaching. All over the country merchants and people were induced to undertake a boycott of Japanese-manufactured goods, just then flooding the markets from which the World War had kept the products of other nations. At first the boycott was not taken very seriously by those against whom it was leveled. Soon, however, a newspaper in Peking, friendly to the Japanese, was writing, "We must confess at this writing that there seems to be something different in the movement which has grown out of popular resentment and despair since the receipt of the verdict from Paris. It appears to be more intelligent, less emotional, better organized, less furious, and, in the first instance, a clearer understanding of causes and a more thorough knowledge of the events which have led up to the calamity."

Soon Japanese steamers on the Yangtze were running without cargoes. Japanese shops in every port were going out of business. In some of the cities, ricksha-pullers would refuse to deposit their passengers before a Japanese place of business. Japanese business fell and fell until it seemed that all the advantage that the war years had brought, when there had been almost no other competitors, would be lost. Day after day a newspaper in Shanghai carried across the top of its first page a statement credited to President Wilson: "A nation boycotted is a nation defeated."

Of course, a thing like that could not go on indefinitely. Nor could the student strike maintain itself long as a worthy political method. In the course of time Japanese goods began to creep back into circulation, and later attempts of the students to dictate to the government by leaving classes, because they had no real popular support, proved a failure. Indeed, it was not long before the student leaders saw the dangers of the strike and turned to other methods. It was too easy to defeat the ends for which the students were in school by leaving classes whenever the authorities did something displeasing. In truth, there were well-grounded suspicions that certain strikes had been deliberately provoked by the militarists in order to give an excuse for the closing of schools that were turning out troublesome graduates.

But the contribution of the Student Movement through that first strike and the subsequent boycott must not be minimized. There were at least three things that it accomplished of far-reaching importance.

For one thing, it stopped the national looting. The years 1916, 1917, 1918, and the first months of 1919, had scarcely seen a month pass without witnessing the signing away of some natural resource that should have meant wealth for China's own sons and daughters. But the outburst of national rage engineered by the students had such a salutary effect that there have been almost no such barters since that date. The strike at least held what was left for China's own possession.

Again, the Student Movement focused public attention on national affairs. It used to be said that, in huge China, with ninety-five per cent of her four hundred million people illiterate, you could not have a public opinion. The students proved that you can. If you go far down in the interior of some of the provinces that lie off the beaten tourist track, you will find painted on city walls the exhortation, "Do not forget the Day of Humiliation." The same words are frequently pressed on cakes, where we would expect to see "Nabisco." And the Day of Humiliation thus held in mind is the one that commemorates the forced acceptance of the Japanese Twenty-One Demands of 1915.

"It was late in the fall of 1919," says Stanley High. "Our party was traveling by coolie caravan across the Chinese province of Kiangsi toward the upper Min River in western Fukien. Finding myself at a river crossing, piled on a ferry with a crowd of chair-bearers, I suggested to a Chinese friend that he ask one of them what he thought of Japan. He did, and, to our amazement, the coolie addressed broke out—as coolies can—into the most violent harangue, at the climax of which he pulled from his tunic a flaring poster depicting Japan as a well-fed thief scurrying away with the rice of starving China." [1]

Things like this you stumble on far from any schools. Their implications can cause you to lose some sleep, for it is no small thing to have such a relentless resentment fostered in the heart of Asia. But they certainly show the success which the Stu-

[1] *The Revolt of Youth,* by Stanley High, Abingdon Press.

dent Movement has had in arousing public interest in national affairs.

Finally, the Movement, as we have already said, brought the student back to his old position of leadership. He has not maintained it since that summer of 1919, at least, in a political way. He has been willing to forgo it for the moment if he may attain it more securely later on. But he then, for the moment, reasserted his place, and showed that, in the forces that will finally mold the new China, he is not to be despised. As a symbol, as well as a concrete achievement, the Student Movement of the summer of 1919 deserves attention.

There are dolorous prophets who say that China is going to pieces. They talk of bandits and *tuchuns* (it is hard to distinguish between them at times) and grafting officials and other marks of a disordered state, and they say that the end is at hand. Perhaps it is, although history tells of other periods when China has been even more disorderly, only to recover her stability and power. But if these prophecies are not fulfilled, and if China does in some way manage to weather the storms that now beset her, she can look back to what happened in 1919, and since then, and thank her students for her salvation.

Without the students, the nation never would have rallied to its own protection. Without the students, a public understanding of the issues at stake would never have been possible. Without the students, the little band of diplomats who cried for justice at the bar of the world's opinion would have been left unsupported. China, in these days of her need, has once more been saved by the men whom she has been wise enough to see are a nation's greatest strength.

It is not sufficient, however, to say that China has been saved by her students, and let it go at that. We must remember that it is a new type of scholar who has done the saving. It is no more the bookworm, the dreamy contemplator of past splendors. It is not the man who came out of the examination stall; it is the man who comes out of the laboratory and the modern classroom. Yes, and the woman; for the girls from their colleges and high schools have borne a full share in this work of national rescue.

The successful assertion of student leadership at the critical moment in 1919 was the great justification, in the Chinese patriot's eyes, of the new type of learning that has supplanted the old. And if anyone doubts that the Chinese now see in this sort of education what they need for the accommodation of their nation to the demands of a new day, let him ponder the growth of the student body in government schools conducted on the new model from 1,625,534 in 1910 to 4,500,000 in 1919. Add the half million students in mission schools, and you have five million Chinese receiving modern education! In less than ten years, filled with disorders

[36]

that would have seemed to make progress impossible, with hardly any money left available by the militarists, the number of Chinese receiving education grew from one in four hundred to one in eighty!

Christians can read those figures, showing as they do the growing confidence in the new type of school and the new type of scholar, with a glow of satisfaction. For it was the Christian missionary who brought that kind of school to China! "Long before Chinese intellectuals themselves ever influenced their countrymen, the missionaries had prepared the ground for them," Dr. Min-chien T. Z. Tyau has written. There are many missionaries still at work in China who can tell of the days when parents had to be paid in order that a handful of cowering, frightened youngsters might be gathered within the sort of schools that had been brought from the West! And today when a thinking Chinese points to a modern school and says, "That is the place from which will come China's saviors," the Christian who has had something to do with first sending that type of education across the Pacific will see more clearly what his gift, directly and indirectly, has meant.

III

A LAND OF FERMENTING MINDS

WHERE were you in the spring of 1916? Were you, by any chance, in New York City? Suppose you had been and suppose some friend had said, "I have tickets for the Columbia commencement. Come on, let's go." Then, as the diplomas were distributed, and a slight young Chinese stepped from a group of his fellow-countrymen to be made a doctor of philosophy, suppose that friend had said, "That young man will influence more lives than any other person now living." Would you not have been sure that your friend was slightly crazy?

So far as I know, nobody made that prophecy at the Columbia commencement in 1916. That young Chinese had crossed two American campuses daily for months without being much distinguished from the other Chinese who were his fellow-students. And today it will seem to some absurd to say that a young man but thirty-two years of age is, or is becoming, the most influential man of our times. Yet, with the possible exception of Mr. Gandhi in India, I think this true. If he lives as long as Mr. Ghandi has, and if his influence keeps expanding in the same degree that it already has, when he dies, Hu Suh will have affected more lives than any other man in this generation.

Should you pick up a copy of *Who's Who in*

POPULAR EDUCATION IS MAKING RAPID STRIDES IN SUCH SCHOOLS
AS THIS, CONDUCTED BY THE Y.W.C.A., WHERE A SIMPLI-
FIED FORM OF WRITING IS BEING TAUGHT

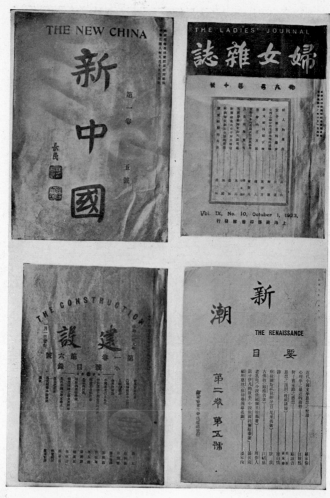

MAGAZINES SYMBOLIC OF CHINA'S REAL REVOLUTION.

China, you would not be likely to pay much attention to the note about Hu Suh. Born in 1892; educated in China and America; a professor in the National University at Peking since 1916; editor of a magazine, *La Jeunesse;* contributor to many other periodicals; author of various books, including a *History of Chinese Philosophy;* member of several educational commissions. That doesn't sound much like the biography of one of the world's most influential men, does it? Nor, but for one fact that lies concealed behind those listed, is it. For Hu Suh is not only a professor of literature in a Chinese university; he is the father of the Chinese Literary Revolution.

When you begin to talk about a Literary Revolution in China, you are swinging clear out of the realm of ideas in which we generally think of the changes that are taking place in that land. Even when we do not think of soldiers and battles and political intrigue, we are likely to think of student mass-meetings and boycotts and soap-box orators. That is to be expected, for, as we said in the previous chapter, it has been that kind of a Student Movement that has saved China from utter disintegration, and has been, in some part, reported in the press of the world.

The political events of the past few years have been a part of China's revolution. But they have been only a part, and not the most important part, at that. The contribution of the students and the educated classes has, to some extent, been made in the political realm. But only to a slight extent. For thinking Chinese have come to see that political change will not be sufficient to make China the land she should be. And the truth is that the students and their leaders have become so sensitive to the shortcomings of political action that they have almost entirely abandoned that form of activity.

We have seen some of the weaknesses of the political agitation of the students; how it took them from the classes in which they were supposed to be learning the things that the country would one day need. Sometimes "direct action" of this kind led, under the excitement of the mob spirit, to excesses that were later bitterly regretted. And always there was the deeper shortcoming that the thoughtful student leader could not overlook, the ignorance of the people, which bound them to habits of thought that made true progress almost impossible.

There was something superb in the courage of the idealists who launched the Chinese Republic in 1911. When Sun Yat-sen and Tang Shao-yi and Li Yuan-hung (all men who had spent student days outside China) started that great adventure, by which China offered herself to light the torch of democracy in the midst of the immemorial darkness of Asiatic autocracy, all the Western world thrilled. How incredible it seemed on that day when we opened our newspapers to learn that the Peacock Throne and the Dragon Flag had been banished forever!

But it takes more than the vision and courage of a few leaders to make a democracy successful. No matter what other circumstances there may be, the power of a people's government depends upon the ability of the people to know what the questions are that face their country and to decide those questions with a fair degree of understanding. That is why, to many Americans, the "little red schoolhouse" has come to be the symbol of their country's greatness, and likewise why some other democratic ventures, in countries with high rates of illiteracy, have not been notably successful.

Think what that meant in China! Here were four hundred million people, only five per cent of whom could read and write. Here learning was a hidden thing, requiring at least a score of years for its discovering. Here was hardly the haziest notion on the part of the masses of the nature of the world in which their new government must take its place. Here were the long-lingering effects of a Great Wall, beyond which new ideas had been kept at bay, and within which old ideas had been preserved long after they should have been discarded. Just a little consideration of such a situation as that will show that, to attempt to establish a democracy on such a foundation, far from guaranteeing benefit, might lead directly to most awful abuses. In fact, the history of the past ten years in China shows plenty of such abuses. If they are to grow less in the future, it will be because the

[41]

character of the public mind has begun to change.

That is what the Republic requires if it is to have any chance for permanency in China—changed minds. John Dewey, one of America's clearest thinkers, saw that after he had been in China just a little while. "The real problem of the Pacific," he wrote to men who were grandiosely talking of that problem in political terms, "the real problem of the Pacific is the problem of the transformation of the mind of China, of the capacity of the oldest and most complicated civilization of the globe to re-make itself into the new forms required by the impact of immense alien forces."

China's student leaders saw this long before Dr. Dewey gave it expression. As far back as 1898 a famous viceroy, Chang Chih-tung, published a book that has been translated as *China's Only Hope*, in which he pleaded for national education. The book had an enormous circulation, and was publicly commended by the emperor. Hardly had the Student Movement of 1919 burst out when thinkers began to call for something more fundamental. "We must change people's minds," they said. "It is not enough to punish our unworthy politicians. We must dig to the very roots of our civilization and transform the forces that make for social stagnation."

But how are you to change the minds of people who cannot read? China had the highest rate of illiteracy of any civilized country. But five per cent of her population could understand the *wen-li*, as the literary style of writing is known. And when you discovered the intricacies of that form of writing, involving at least twenty years of unremitting study for its mastery, you wondered, not that there were so few who could read it, but that twenty million could! Think of trying to re-make the mind of a quarter of the human race with an instrument as dismayingly ineffective as *wen-li!*

Did you ever notice the way in which Mr. H. G. Wells ran on to this disturbing fact? Turn to one of the most engaging parts of his *Outline of History*. Here he comes, tripping down the centuries, cracking a head here and a tradition there, stopping from time to time to fish a moral from the various sloughs of despond into which we have flung ourselves, but always managing to keep faith in the future alive, to keep marching toward a millennium, and almost reaching it when he runs, slap!—into the Chinese language. It is a jarring experience for Mr. Wells, and he shows it by devoting more space to it than he does to the American Civil War. Nor can you blame him. For Mr. Wells is entirely right. As long as the Chinese written language remained what it was when Mr. Wells was writing, it stood as an impenetrable barrier between a quarter of the race and an understanding of their age. And while that condition continued, as it had for thousands of years, any hope for Mr. Wells's millennium was vain.

[43]

What sort of a language is this *wen-li*? Thousands of years ago it began as the ordinary language of speech as well as of writing. But, as the centuries passed, it was refined and refined by the sages in their writing. Confucius, who lived five hundred years before Christ, found it a perfected vehicle for his books. It has no alphabet, of course. The Chinese use ideographs (picture symbols) rather than the arbitrary *a b c* with which we are familiar. But even the ideographs, known as characters, were no longer used in their primary meaning. A character became attached in thought to some famous idea in which it had been used by some sage, until the point has been reached whereby one character stands for a half dozen or more words. Reading, therefore, becomes the art of remembering numberless literary allusions, to which characters, often with little reference to their primary meaning, give the clue.

It is simply impossible to give a satisfactory illustration in English of the way in which *wen-li* is written. We have, in the West, no literature, even including that of ancient Egypt, comparable to it. But suppose Shakespeare had written twenty-five hundred years ago. And suppose his line, "The quality of mercy is not strained," had made a deep impression as a perfect expression of one literary idea. Suppose others, coming after, had wanted to reproduce it, but without writing it in full. Suppose they had just written "quality," without reference to whether it meant quality in persons or in goods. Then suppose the same process had been repeated with the next line, the key-word this time being "dew" which would be indistinguishable from "do" or "due." And suppose now that when you came to pick up a paper and saw there two characters, "quality" and "dew," you were expected immediately to think of some such lofty expression as, "The exercise of mercy is one of the most worthy acts that heaven has ever inspired in the hearts of men." There you would have, if you can think of such an unthinkable way of writing as that, some faint approximation of the sort of a written language *wen-li* is.

You don't wonder that not many Chinese can read *wen-li,* do you? More than a hundred years before Christ, petitions addressed to the throne stated that the *wen-li* had become unintelligible to the majority of the public officials. Indeed, it was the discovery that his officers could not read his mandates that made the emperor install the system of literary examinations, insuring that the public officials should be chosen from men who could.

The spoken language of most of China, however, is no such bugaboo. In fact, it is one of the simplest languages used by any civilized people. Without declensions or conjugations, it might almost be said to be without grammar. Yet it is pungent and pithy, and capable of infinite variations and shadings. In parts of South China it has, in the course of the centuries, with the absence of easy intercommunication, become radically different from the spoken language of North and Central China. But, roughly speaking, there may be said to be at least three hundred million Chinese using some form of what is known as the Mandarin, or *kuan-hwa* dialect.

The relation between the written *wen-li* and the spoken Mandarin (*kuan-hwa*) has been compared to that which existed in Europe in medieval times between Latin and the vulgar tongues. The comparison is not a bad one. For just as in medieval Europe there existed one language for literature and the talk of scholars and courts, with other languages for the speech of the common people that might have grown out of the Latin but were no longer recognizable as its offspring, so in China the *wen-li* and the *kuan-hwa* have lived beside each other. And just as in Europe Dante and Chaucer and Luther and others had to begin to write a literature in Italian and English and German before there could come the great awakening of the Renaissance and the Reformation, so in China men had to begin to read and write as they spoke before any popular mental awakening could be possible.

Centuries ago some Chinese perceived this, and started to write in the vernacular. Not with any strange symbols, be it understood. The same historic characters were employed, but in their everyday significance. And a character meant what it plainly said, "only that and nothing more." Yet these attempts had only a restricted success. Certain novels written in the *kuan-hwa* achieved a wide reading, and the later experiments of Christian missionaries with a Mandarin version of the Bible gave the gospel to large numbers who could never have read it in the *wen-li*. Such departures from precedent awoke the derision of all the *literati*.

"What! do you call that real Chinese literature?" they would scoff, pointing at one of the offending novels. "That's not literature; that's just trash, just words strung together to while away time for a tea-room lounger."

And when the Mandarin Bible was mentioned, their scorn was even more blighting.

"That a Chinese book? That's not a book; that's just another sample of the foreigner's barbarism. Think of saying that the maxims contained in any such hodge-podge of style as that are to be compared with the words of our sages! Why, any farmer could understand that!"

And then Dr. Hu Suh, whom we have almost forgotten since we saw him receiving his diploma in the first paragraph of this chapter, appeared on the scene. As a professor in the National University at Peking, Dr. Hu found himself a member of a group of professors noted for their independence, their keenness of mind, and their patriotism. Soon he found the whole faculty in agreement that no Student Movement nor other such political activity could avail for the salvation of China until some way were found of reaching and changing the minds of China's common people. And when he suggested that the attempt be made to reach that mind by writing in a way more understandable than the *wen-li*, Dr. Hu discovered his colleagues ready to support him.

This university group had been publishing a little monthly magazine known as *Youth*, or *La Jeunesse*. This magazine Dr. Hu used as the weapon for his attack on the ancient form of writing. He published an article entitled "Suggestions for the Reform of Chinese Literature," in which he made the proposal that, in order to make knowledge democratic, Chinese should be written as the best *kuanhwa* is spoken.

"If we truly wish to give China a literature which shall not only be expressive of the real life and thoughts of our own time, but also an effective force in intellectual and social reforms," Dr. Hu wrote, "we must first emancipate ourselves from the fetters of a dead language which may once have been the literary instrument for our forefathers, but which certainly is not adequate for the creation of a living literature of our times. It is to free ourselves from these shackles that we are now proposing the adoption of spoken Chinese as our literary medium."

To the new style of writing was generally given the name of *pei-hwa*, or "white language," which is an expressive Chinese idiom meaning "plain language." The "white" hints at the whiteness of sunlight, in the full glare of which nothing can be hidden. It is a sort of Oriental way of suggesting what we Westerners would call "language that can be seen through," although the Oriental idiom seems even more vigorous and suggestive.

When first the *pei-hwa* appeared, it was greeted with a howl of derision. What sort of an assumption of learning was this? But derision did not stop Dr. Hu and his friends. They went ahead, writing all sorts of things in the new form. They translated articles from Western periodicals dealing with matters of immense moment; they recounted bits of Chinese history; they even dared attempt poetry! And other publications began to appear in other student centers, written in the same novel style.

From derision, the old-time scholars passed to the most violent opposition. Use of the *pei-hwa* was denounced as treason to the most sacred traditions of China's history. Confucius, Mencius, and all the other makers of China's civilization had written *wen-li;* who were these who would displace it? Certainly they could not be one hundred per cent Chinese!

So the struggle went on, at the same time that the political activities of the students were attracting so much attention. Finally, Dr. Hu brought it to a focus in a typically Chinese fashion.

There is probably no more rational being than the Chinese. He is not like the traditional Scotchman, who is reputed to have said that he was open to conviction, but that he would like to meet the man who could convince him! The Chinese is generally open to conviction, and it requires only a demonstration that appeals to his innate reasoning powers to convince him. He can be more easily reached by a logical statement than most men. To a large extent this is a part of the magnificent heritage left him by Confucius.

Dr. Hu felt that a rational demonstration of the capability of the *pei-hwa* to express *any* sort of thought would decide the battle between the old and new forms of writing. So he set himself the most exacting literary task that he could conceive. He wrote, and a progressive Chinese firm published, a two-volume *History of Chinese Philosophy*. It was in the new form, and the reading public, after admitting its excellency, also had to admit that if the *pei-hwa* could successfully express all the niceties of thought that had marked all the sages of all the ages, it could express anything. The book became, and has remained, a best seller. And with its acceptance, the battle for the *pei-hwa* was won.

All over China magazines in the new form began to pour from the presses. Wherever two or three students were gathered together, there they generally founded a new paper. Many of these died with a few issues, but others prospered. The newspapers almost universally abandoned the *wen-li*, and the majority of the books appeared in the *pei-hwa*. The circulation of all papers went up, for the simpler form made it possible for thousands to read who had been debarred by the old classical style. Thousands of Chinese knew enough characters to read ordinary news, provided that news was written in the style where a character meant what it did when used in speech. At a conservative estimate, the introduction of the *pei-hwa* must have more than doubled the Chinese reading public since the close of the World War. Some would say that it has been tripled. And the rate of increase continues, for it is now possible, by using this new form, to give a child the rudiments of an education—the readin' and 'ritin', if not the 'rithmetic—in three or four years of school. It is easily conceivable that, within fifty years, if there is a fair degree of public order, China can have a citizenship at least as literate as that of many of the countries of Europe. And it is the thought of this great horde to whom the horizons of knowledge have been thus suddenly broadened that makes us say, as we did at the beginning, that the unassuming little professor who was a student in our American colleges only a few years ago may ultimately influence more lives than any other person now living.

To us, interested as we are in the fate of Christianity in China, there is an especial import in this victory for the *pei-hwa*. For since those pioneer days when the Bible, despite the jeers of the *literati*, was translated into the vernacular, the Christian writer in China has experimented in writing in this

[51]

form. Now the despised vernacular becomes the literary fashion, and millions of new hands are stretching out for reading matter. It is the day of all days for the printing-press in China. If the Christian forces are wise enough to enlist such of their young Chinese leaders as are capable in the production of literature in this new form, the progress of the Christian message should take on unexampled speed.

Of course, this fundamental problem of transforming the mind of China is not solved when you work out a system of writing that the masses can understand. If you have not something worth saying, to what profit is all the turmoil?

Many of us have gasped in admiration in recent months as we have watched a tiny aeroplane scud across the sky and write letters a half mile high upon the heavens. But I think that most of us, as we have seen those letters form into nothing more than the name of a cheap cigarette, have felt that we were watching a gigantic display of misdirected energy. John Ruskin told England when the first cable was laid to India, "You have only wasted an all-around-the-world's length of copper wire. . . . If you had had, perchance, two words of common sense to say, though you had taken wearisome time and trouble to send them, the two words of common sense would have been worth the carriage, and more."

The reformers who have sponsored the *pei-hwa*

in China have seen and escaped this danger. From
the first they have relied principally upon the content of their message to carry its form. They have
dealt with the most searching problems in Chinese
life; they have translated the latest thinking of the
outstanding minds of the West. There has never
been a time when the news-stands that bore *pei-hwa*
literature did not, by that fact, guarantee that they
were selling the most up-to-date, thoughtful, and
helpful writing in China.

As an example of the scope of interest on the part
of these pioneers, take the table of contents of a
single issue of three different magazines. These are
just ordinary issues, such as might be found at any
time in any one of the student centers of China.
They have been largely written by the faculties and
students of certain government schools. Compare
them with the papers that Western students publish.

The Renaissance

The Christ Before Jesus
The Foundations of Anarchy, and the Society of Anarchy
Opposed to the Life of Individualism
The Field of Psychology
Industry in Relation to Livelihood
Woman's Rights and the Law
The Present-day Power of Democracy
The Building of Public Opinion
The Methods of Sociology

CHINA'S REAL REVOLUTION

La Jeunesse

Pragmatism
The Foundations of Russian Revolutionary Philosophy
Work in Relation to Life
Discussing the Foundations of Electoral Franchise
Revolution in Thought
Men's and Women's Social Relations Should Be Free

Emancipation and Reconstruction

Leadership, Competition, and the Labor Movement
Labor Unions
A Criticism of Socialism
Biological Egoism, Altruism, and Universal Love
The Education of Commercial Apprentices
The Logical Leadership of the Labor Movement
Lenin and Trotsky—The Men and Their Ideas
The Definition of Socialism

Do you notice how many times the word "foundations" appears in that short list of articles? In a way that symbolizes the mental revolution in China, of which the work of Dr. Hu Suh is a part. For the enthusiasm and the devotion by which, in the face of the most vituperative opposition, Dr. Hu and his followers changed in five years the cultural outlook of millions of Chinese can only be explained as we see this so-called Literary Revolution as a foundation for something larger.

This larger movement is an intellectual upheaval to which the Chinese have given the suggestive name

PASTOR TING LI-MEI, ONE OF THE LEADERS IN BUILDING THE CHRISTIANITY OF CHINA'S FUTURE, WHICH WILL BE A CHINESE CHRISTIANITY EXPRESSED BY CHINESE MINDS.

of the New Tide of Thought. Sometimes it is spoken of as the New Civilization Movement; sometimes as the New Thought Movement; sometimes as the Renaissance. But the first name seems most graphically to characterize it. It is the sweeping in of a great new tide of thinking, calculated to wash away all the superstitions and wrong ideas that have hampered progress in the past, and to leave only the social customs and beliefs that can stand firm even when deep waters swirl about them.

In the long run, as China's clearest thinking patriots see, the stability of the Republic will depend upon a society that is not only literate, but in harmony with all modern wisdom. This has impelled student leaders, and other like-minded Chinese, to begin to study most relentlessly all the social customs, educational methods, and popular beliefs, in order to find out what are and what are not worthy to survive in this new day.

"The Movement," said a book written by some of its leaders recently, "has put up as its platform four big tasks; namely, the reorganization, the re-statement, and the re-evaluation of Chinese civilization with critical examination of it; a thorough and scientific study of theories and facts; a reconstruction of individual and social life." [1]

No crusader ever set out to win the Holy City with any deeper sense of consecration to a great

[1] *China Today Through Chinese Eyes.* By four Chinese, of whom Dr. Hu Suh is one. George H. Doran Co., New York.

spiritual task than these young Chinese have felt as they have undertaken this adventure. When we consider how any achievement of its purposes would alter some of the very bases of the life of four hundred million people, we are the more amazed at their courage. And, of course, it will be a long time before their goals are fully attained. Yet it is marvelous what they have already accomplished. Largely, this is because of the methods that they have adopted.

"Science as a method," says one of the Christian leaders of the movement, "is strongly advocated and persistently followed. . . . Nothing is to be accepted unless it can stand the tests of the scientific method. . . . The movement has been a relentless foe to despotic government and autocratic institutions of every sort. . . . The movement lays the emphasis upon relentless thoroughness. The movement has thus far proved to be one which has unusual courage and persistency. No obstacle is too great to overcome, and no compromise is small enough to be tolerated. . . . There is nothing too radical for examination. Convention and traditions have lost their prestige. Time-honored practices, if in any way they do not meet the exigencies of the present day, are to be cast aside, root and branch, altogether. Proprieties and customs which have ruled for centuries give way unless they can withstand the challenge that is being put to them." [1]

[1] Ibid.

So it is that, all over China, students and other thinkers are turning from the confusion of the political scene to examine the underlying facts of the national life out of which the political scene grows. And as these customs, sanctions, and beliefs are discovered, they are made to answer a threefold examination: What is this? Why is this? What value has this for to-day?

Religion must answer these questions as well as the other aspects of Chinese life, and this means not only the religions of the past—Taoism, Buddhism, Mohammedanism, and Confucianism—but this new religion that has made such progress in a century, Christianity. Searching indeed have been some of the questionings put to Christianity by thinking Chinese during the last two or three years. Some earnest people have been greatly alarmed to see their faith thus under fire. But they need not have been. Christianity fears no honest examination, and these leaders in the Chinese Renaissance are honest. In fact, if the apostle Paul could walk in China to-day and study the methods of the New Tide of Thought, he would probably say that these workers for a new day are but carrying out the injunction he made long ago, "Prove all things; hold fast that which is good."

Every school becomes a center for this sort of intellectual and social ferment. And with schools increasing at the rate that they are in China, this means that the New Tide of Thought is constantly flowing into new communities. It is rare, indeed, to find a large center now that has not felt its influence, and the two hundred magazines devoted to its purposes are carrying its message where even its living exponents have not gone.

Nor is it to be thought that the supporters of the Movement confine themselves to discussions of theory. They are carrying their theories into practice, and their examples are more powerful in influencing popular opinion than any amount of argument could be. When a man whose mind commands respect says that the age-old burial customs, with their accompanying burden of expense that may tax several generations, are not fit for the present, and then buries his parents in a quiet, unostentatious manner that gives no hint of any lessening of filial piety, it is nearly sure to follow that there will be other funerals of the same kind in that locality. And when a girl who has had unusual educational advantages refuses to be bound by the old methods of match-making, but chooses her life-mate herself from those who can afford her mental comradeship, all the matrimonial go-betweens in the neighborhood foresee the ultimate doom of their profession. So it goes.

If you look at the outer aspects of Chinese life today, the picture is gloomy. The country presents the aspect of a huge, unwieldy machine, out of all control, falling to pieces, and endangering all about as it goes to ruin. But when you look below this

outer aspect and see the workings of such a movement as the New Tide of Thought, you regain hope.
Such a movement cannot hope to achieve its ends
in a few months. It is a process that will require
much time for discovery and correction. But the
leaders who have forsaken present political activity
in order that they may ultimately change the civilization of the people, have chosen wisely. If they
can maintain and attain their purposes, no man can
put bounds on the future that lies before their
country.

This is China's real revolution, this fermentation
of the minds of the Chinese. This, and not the warfare and brigandage, is what you must study if you
would know the China that is to be. And it is our
purpose now, therefore, to consider in four relationships the way in which this true revolution is coming to pass. In the realms of social customs,
womanhood, industry, and religion, what changes
are taking place?

IV

"PROVE ALL THINGS"

ONCE upon a time there lived in China a poor man with one son. I have forgotten the poor man's name and the son's name, but we will call them Wang. Almost anybody in China who isn't named Li is named Wang. Likewise, at that time, and ever since then, in fact, there lived in China a horde of mosquitoes. Old Mr. Wang, being a poor man, had not the money wherewith to buy himself a mosquito net for his bed, so that the pests would hold a celebration each night after he had retired, to the detriment of the unfortunate man's repose. At last, things reached such a pass that something radical had to be done, or old Mr. Wang would have been numbered with his ancestors. So young Wang— he was really only a boy—dutifully lay in the bed for an hour or more each evening until the mosquitoes had gorged themselves on him. Then his father could sleep the rest of the night in peace.

That story, with added details, has been told to hundreds of Chinese youngsters, and the sacrifice of young Wang—or whatever his name was—has been held up during generations as an ideal illustration of the working of the greatest of all Chinese virtues, filial piety. As far as I know, the story never said much about the way in which the boy spent the hours after he had finished furnishing a feast for the mosquitoes. For no Chinese would ever think of asking about the boy. Social custom for millenniums has decreed that the first business in life is to show deference to parents, and it is only in these days of China's inner revolution that some radicals are beginning to suggest that there may be others with rights in such cases.

The maze of social custom that has bound the old China is bewildering to a visitor from the West. To reach a banquet and then see the master of ceremonies argue with some guest for ten or fifteen minutes over the place in which the guest is to sit, may seem amusing or a useless waste of time, according to one's hunger. The master of ceremonies will ask a guest to sit in a certain chair; the guest will say that he is totally unworthy of that chair, and start toward a less honorable one; the master of ceremonies will repudiate the suggestion and renew the first invitation; the guest will again show reluctance. And so on and on and on, until what is to the foreigner an invisible point has been reached, the proprieties properly satisfied and the guest takes the chair which he has known all the time he would take and which he would have been mortally offended if he had not been given, as the master of ceremonies well knew.

These social customs have, of course, been a growth of ages. When our civilization is as old as China's, we may have as many conventions to which to defer. Many think we have enough as it is.

But it is astonishing to discover that most of these ideas and sanctions were fixed more than two thousand years ago! One of the books that comes down from the time of Confucius is known as the *Book of Rites,* and what detailed rules for conduct were not crowded into that classic will be found in some other of the great sage's writings. Confucius wanted everything done decently and in order. He was a ritualist if ever one lived. The legislature of Oklahoma has been held up to ridicule in some quarters for passing on the proper length of hotel bed-sheets. But Confucius went the Oklahoma legislators one better. He meticulously described the proper method for getting into bed and out again after the sheets had been spread!

The old type of education in China, which consisted in committing to memory the classics, must have had a striking resemblance to the new education that Americans are being urged to undertake by the advertisements that ask, "What is wrong with this picture?" The difference has been that, in China, sitting in the presence of one's parents, or such a matter, has not been regarded as merely a social blunder, but as a sign of moral turpitude.

It is this kind of a social heritage that the inner revolution, the New Tide of Thought, that we mentioned in the previous chapter, is judging. It is taking all these social customs and sanctions, putting them to the tests suggested by the needs of the present day, and attempting the enormous task of telling the Chinese people which ones to discard and which ones to alter and which ones to observe unchanged. For when this movement attempts to "prove all things," it must accept the social manners of the people as among the most important elements in the national life.

Rudyard Kipling once compressed into four lines the secret of his ability to understand and interpret life:

> I keep six honest serving men
> (They taught me all I knew);
> Their names are What, and Why, and When,
> And How, and Where, and Who.

The men who are carrying on China's inner revolution ask much the same questions. Mr. Basil Mathews, the English editor, has said of China today:

"Everything is challenged on the earth and in the heavens: religion, marriage, family affection, respect of son for father or pupil for teacher or servant for master.

"All the palings are down. No taboos are held sacred. Every stone is overturned. Nothing has any authority until it has been accepted by the individual judgment.

"All despotisms are despised. . . .

"Every presupposition of the past is challenged with a rather strident and quite insistent 'Why?' It [the New Thought Movement] is a stupendous *enfant terrible* in a three-thousand-year-old house. . . .

"It is out to rebuild the social order from the very foundations. It is after a new order at any cost."

This challenging of the former ways of living might not produce such a strain were it not for the fundamental assumption upon which all Chinese society is built. This assumption makes the family, and not the individual, the social unit. A man has meaning, in Chinese eyes, only as a part of a family or clan. The honor that comes to one comes also to the family. On the other hand, if one person goes wrong, the stigma alights upon the whole group. The family, for example, is considered as liable for debts contracted by any of its members.

Because this is so, the social practices of the past have been calculated to bind the family ever more closely together. One did not reverence ancestors just for the sake of reverencing ancestors, but as an acknowledgment of the unbroken family life. And one submitted to a choice of wife or husband by parents, not because one had no interest in the matter, but because it was the interest of the family that must be first taken into account. So through all the range of social customs.

Now the New Tide of Thought declares that the individual must be the center of interest. You as you, and not merely as one of a great group of people all bearing the same surname, must become a contributing factor in the state. You must be held individually responsible, and because of that, you must not be required to submit to any line of conduct that does not appeal to your own best judgment. You therefore have the right to take up any social practice and ask whether or not it is best to act in conformity with it in the present day.

To the mass of Chinese, steeped in the idea of the power of the family, any suggestion of undermining family authority seems the most dreadful sort of impiety. "The family life of China," they will tell you, "has worked out a system, through more than forty centuries, whereby people can get along with each other in peace. It may have had minor imperfections, but on the whole it has brought happiness. No well-wisher of China would attack our family institutions."

Yet that is just what the leaders of the New Thought Movement are doing. They deny boldly that Chinese family life has been ideal, and that its customs should accordingly persist unchanged. Early last year a British correspondent interviewed Dr. Hu Suh, and later reported in a newspaper published in Japan that Dr. Hu had said:

"The Chinese family system is bad. People talk about the harmony of the Chinese family and the Chinese village. It is all nonsense. If I should go to my home village now, the people would come to tell me of their squabbles and probably would fight with one another at my gate. There is constant discord. It is a bad system."

So, believing that not only the forms, but the very spirit of the family life of old China is unfitted to furnish the basis of a strong modern state, the reformers have begun to bring changes in the structure. It is surprising to see some of the changes that appear to be coming in Chinese family relationships, but it must be remembered that these have been proposed only after the former ways had been submitted to the most honest appraisal.

Take the matter of betrothal as an example. Child betrothal has been exceedingly common in China, and even when this did not occur, the arrangement has been one of convenience between the families rather than the individuals immediately concerned. It frequently happened that betrothed couples did not see each other until the hour of their wedding. Certain individuals made quite a profitable business out of the arrangement of marriages, and there was almost none of the personal selection and courtship that, in the West, have seemed so precious.

Yet there were some things to be said for Chinese practice. "It may be hard for the romantic Westerner to conceive of conjugal love existing where it never had a chance to grow or develop," Dr. M. T. Z. Tyau has written, "but in view of the fact that separations and divorces are practically unknown in the unemotional East, it is not so impossible as is generally imagined. Has not somebody suggested that if we put two people of the opposite sex together alone, however unattractive they both may be, in the end they will be mutually attracted to each other? . . . Moreover, all parents are reasonable and wish their children joy. So while some may arrange their children's marriages with an eye to the prospective bride or groom's position or wealth, despite the utter incompatibility of the two young people, such cannot be predicated in the preponderating majority of cases. In their own light, therefore, the parents will arrange the most suitable alliances; then the children will live happily, and parents, though deceased, will be reverenced as in actual life." [1]

The modern Chinese thinker, however, while admitting that the old system has a better record in the matter of divorce than the Western, is not content to abide by the ancient customs. He demands the right to pick his own life-mate, and to pick her —or him, as the case may be—from the number of those who can live upon the same intellectual plane.

Many a teacher in a mission school could tell of experiences when students have reported their betrothal to boys or girls with whom they had no intellectual or other sympathy. Chafing under the condition, the students will ask the foreigner to help them win release from their obligations. Perhaps the foreigner attempts to do so—once. After that he realizes that questions such as these the Chinese

[1] Tyau, M. T. Z. *China Awakened*. Macmillan Co., New York.

[67]

must work out for themselves. But there is frequently something pathetic in the way in which these youngsters seek escape from customs which reach from out the past to clutch them. Especially is this the case when their religious faith is involved. The Christian preacher who has been handicapped by an uneducated wife from a non-Christian home whom he felt forced to marry because of a childhood betrothal has been too frequent a figure in the Chinese Church. And many a girl has gone from a Christian school to marriage with a non-Christian man, feeling that her soul-health was endangered by the act.

You can see that filial piety is closely related to this question. The young Chinese who refuses to accept a betrothal made by his or her parents is not only in rebellion against hoary convention, but is popularly condemned for showing a want of filial devotion. And that is the worst sin that can be charged against a Chinese. Many of the thinkers of today are saying that China's stability has been, in large measure, an answer to the promise of the Decalog: "Honor thy father and thy mother, that thy days may be long in the land." They realize, therefore, that in advocating lines of conduct that seemingly undermine parental authority radicals are embarking upon a dangerous course.

In one of the cities of China there was, until a year or so ago, a young Chinese woman who had earned great prominence as an executive of a Christian organization. Well educated, her natural ability brought her rapidly to the front among the constructive workers of that city. But there came a time when she seemed to lose interest in her work. She moped about her office until finally a foreign associate asked her if she were not feeling well. Then the whole story came out.

The girl had been betrothed by her family to a man in another city. The man was not a Christian, and the girl knew nothing of him personally. She had held out for months against such a marriage, but the weight of family opinion was heavily set against her. At last, her mother, who had been unusually forbearing, told her that she would regard any further refusal as a lack of filial devotion, and the result of her Christian associations.

As much to show that Christianity did *not* require its followers to repudiate their distinctively Chinese ideas, as for any other reason, the girl finally married the groom selected for her by her parents. And to her joy, her husband, while not a Christian, has encouraged her in her devotion to her faith, so that she has been able to continue to bear an outstanding part in the work of the church. Not all are so fortunate.

What the final outcome will be, it is impossible to say. It seems improbable that the staid Oriental will ever adopt the promiscuous courtship of the West. In fact, some recent radical proposals arising out of the student circles, such as the introduction

[69]

of "free love," are likely to produce a reaction toward conservatism. But in the long run the reformers, if successful, will secure some sort of basis for the formation of the family that does not so largely ignore the feelings of those most involved.

When it comes to the celebration of marriage rites the changes again are many. The leaders of the Renaissance are not opposed to the old ceremonies because of any lack of beauty, because there was a dignity about some of the marriage rites that was profoundly impressive. But marriages frequently involved a cost that was out of all relation to the means of the family, and left a burden of debt of staggering proportions. To meet this debt the custom grew of requiring wedding guests to contribute heavily, which was as hard on the guests as it might otherwise have been on the family.

It was never my fortune to attend one of the old-style weddings in China. Sometimes I have seen the heavily decorated and curtained bridal carriage or sedan chair before the door of the bride's home, and have seen the bride in her crimson gown, with the pink veil across her face, come forth for her ride to her new home, with all her dowry—furniture, dress-stuffs, clocks, and the wedding feast—following behind her.

Friends have told me of those ceremonies, with the couple bowing the required number of times before each pair of parents, before the ancestral

[70]

IT MAKES ALL THE DIFFERENCE IN THE WORLD ON WHICH SIDE OF
THE FENCE ONE STANDS—WHEN ON THE OTHER SIDE IS
A MISSION PLAYGROUND.

FAMILIAR SIGHTS IN CHINA'S FUNERAL PROCESSIONS: A DWELLING
AND ATTENDANTS, WHICH WILL BE BURNED AT THE GRAVE
FOR THE USE OF THE DEAD IN THE SPIRIT WORLD.

tablets, before the household gods, before the professional go-betweens who arranged the match, and before the guests. Then came the climactic moment, when the veil was thrown back and the groom, perhaps for the first time, saw his wife. There must have been plenty of weddings when the unveiling provided anything but a happy surprise. Indeed, my wife happened once to be a guest at a state wedding, when the groom took no pains to hide his rage at the disclosure of the somewhat ample features of the bride whom his parents had secured for him.

Great were the feastings that invariably followed, and the buffoonery that broke out must have been terrifying to the poor girl who was its victim. Yet custom decreed that if she, by so much as a glance, gave any indication of annoyance, she should be regarded as lacking in matronly poise.

The festivities connected with weddings held in humble homes near my own frequently lasted for the better part of a week, and must have left all the participants unfit for any real work for some time after that.

All sorts of attempts are being made nowadays to work out a form of marriage that will be inexpensive, solemn, Chinese in spirit, and without the boisterous and sometimes repulsive horseplay formerly indulged in. Thus, Dr. Tyau tells of the marriage of two students who had studied outside China. The ceremony followed this order:

[71]

1. Music.
2. The guests were seated.
3. The witness took up his position.
4. The go-betweens took their positions.
5. The best man escorted the groom to the witness.
6. The bridesmaids escorted the bride to the witness.
7. Music.
8. The witness read the marriage certificate.
9. The groom put the ring on the bride's finger.
10. The bride and bridegroom bowed to each other twice.
11. The bride and bridegroom bowed to the witness.
12. The bride and bridegroom bowed to the go-betweens.
13. The bride and bridegroom bowed to the guests. The guests arose to return the bow.
14. The bride and bridegroom bowed three times to their relatives.
15. Music.

The ceremony in this case, it will be seen, was in charge of an official witness. The certificate read:

T. L. K. of Chihli Province, and S. J. S. of Chekiang Province, having agreed to be married to each other, are today, the 28th day of June, 1918, united in wedlock before the witness T. Y. P. The affections of the two are overflowing and will continue though their hairs turn gray.

(Signed)   T. Y. P., T. L. K., S. J. S., S. C.

In the case of Christians there is also an attempt to combine the ceremonies that the churches of the West have evolved with ancient Chinese usage. In one wedding in Shanghai the Western form was followed exclusively, save that the groom, seeing the bride approaching down the church aisle, hastened, with his best man, to greet her, and the procession approached the altar four abreast; that, at the close of the ceremony, the newly wedded couple made ceremonial bows to their guests; and that the guests, being unfamiliar with some of the technique of Western weddings, pelted the two with rice as soon as they started to march away from the altar. At the wedding feast that followed this same occasion, an attempt was made to introduce the old-style horse-play, drinking the groom under the table, and the like. But the groom, with a little tact and firmness, quickly stopped this.

More important than rites, if the young Chinese is to be allowed to pick his or her life-mate, is the inculcation of proper standards of choice. It is of more than passing significance to find the *Chinese Ladies Journal* running an article on "Selecting a Husband," and giving voice to sentiments such as these:

"According to modern Chinese custom a son or daughter has the right to make his or her own choice in matrimony without interference from the parents. Chinese, for thousands of years, have followed the custom of having such choice made by the parents instead of by the couples themselves. This bad custom often caused unhappiness, because the parents cared very little for the element of love between the young people. Since Western civilization came

[73]

eastward this custom has gradually changed. Young lovers have often misused the term 'free marriage,' and considerable immorality has resulted.

"Since love should be lifelong, and as there is nothing so fine as love, the marriage of young people should not be decided upon in a hurry. It is necessary to investigate habits and character with great care, so as to avoid future regrets on the part of the contracting parties. The following are the important points for Chinese women to consider in making their choice, and I should like to bring them forth and discuss them with young girls who are looking for husbands."

Then follows a discussion of the necessary list of qualifications, in this order: appearance and knowledge, age, occupation, property, relations, health, living habits, temper, character, purpose, and general considerations. And the editor closes with this exhortation:

"The other points may be learned by interview or by correspondence, or by getting information from his neighbors. If his morals are satisfactory, an engagement may be entered into. In this way you will never regret your action. . . . Don't be too shy to investigate. This is a matter of great importance for your lifelong happiness."

Another social custom that is slowly retreating before the attack of the reformers is that of foot-binding. Here the influence of Christianity has been marked, for the agitation against foot-binding first found expression in Christian circles. It was when the missionaries began to refuse admission to their schools to girls with bound feet that the custom received its first bad setback, and in all the succeeding years the Christians have never let up on this fight.

Just how far this reform has progressed is hard to say. In some parts of the country the women on the farms have never been cursed with the deformity. In most of the port cities there are few girls or young women whose feet are bound. But in the interior cities and other out-of-the-way parts of China, the bound foot still flourishes. A friend of mine who traveled in progressive Shansi Province a year ago reports that he did not see a single female, save infants, without bound feet. The students, however, maintain that the custom is passing everywhere, and will soon disappear.

A more serious problem is that presented by concubinage. It is hard to say whether the leaders of the New Tide have reached any clear stand on this question as yet, although there are many individuals who have come out strongly against the custom. Concubinage, it should be understood, arises generally out of the desire for male offspring, and is sometimes urged upon a husband by his wife when there are no male children to carry on the family name. It is considered a terrible thing in China to allow a family to die out.

Christianity has also found it difficult to deal with this question. Almost all churches refuse baptism to men with more than one wife, but this has necessitated keeping out sincere converts who have felt that, in view of the social disgrace involved, it would be unjust to turn out secondary wives taken before their conversion. I well remember a teacher of Chinese, whose secondary wife was keeping him out of church membership, who could not see why he should be required to put her away while Abraham, Moses, David, and other Old Testament worthies were being held up to him as patterns of faith and piety!

It is certain, however, that the New Tide will have to deal with this question. At present, it is embarrassed by the action of some students who, having studied abroad, and returning to China to find family-chosen brides without education awaiting them, have seen in a second marriage a solution for the dilemma. Such students have married the first wife to satisfy family claims and the second to find a real life-mate. These cases have been, however, comparatively rare.

In the long run, the New Tide will insist that concubinage go. It cannot stand up before that insistent "Why?" It brings discord into too many homes. Monogamy proves itself, by the best scientific tests, the only sure basis for a country.

Somewhat connected with the custom of concubinage is that of holding household slaves. Many Chinese will insist that "slave" is too strong a word to use in this connection, since the girl is only held during her girlhood. But it must be admitted that the girls sold by their needy families to work for more prosperous ones do live in virtual slavery. The end of their years of labor may be marriage, or it may be concubinage, or it may be far worse. And during the years of bondage the girl servant is as much a chattel as though she were in prison.

Household slavery in China has recently attracted attention in the West because the custom, naturally, had found a foothold in the British colony of Hongkong. The matter was brought to the attention of the House of Commons, quick to uphold the boast that where the Union Jack floats all men are free. In Hongkong itself the agitation had large Christian and Chinese backing, although it must be confessed that some of the foreigners with business interests in the city were very slow in lending support. The law as finally passed provided that on January 1, 1923, all household slaves should be freed. The thrusting of this great crowd of young girls on their own resources in such a city has placed a heavy tax upon the Christian and student leaders. Agitation will now go forward to extend this reform to other parts of China.

It would be easy to devote this entire chapter to the changes that are coming in the burial customs of China. Burial seems always to have occupied a large place in Chinese life. Perhaps that is because of the high death-rate, with the average expectation of life, if one is lucky enough to be one of the thirty per cent or so who survive infancy, being only something like twenty-four years. In every part of the country there are great tracts, frequently very valuable land, given over to graves. One passes them in such numbers that one comes to sympathize with the man who said that what China needed was the gospel of cremation!

The Chinese funeral has become a most expensive affair. In some parts of the country it may last for months, with frequent ceremonies attendant upon the varnishing of a casket or upon the return of Buddhist and Taoist priests for another period of chanting. There are grandsons in China today who are eating the bitterness of grinding poverty in an attempt to pay the funeral expenses of their grandfathers.

In the city of Changsha, near the center of China, where the medical school and college supported by Yale University is located, there is a little Christian servant whose name, appropriately enough, is Valiant One. For months the child had been trying to interest her family in the religion she had found in the mission church, when suddenly her eldest sister's little son and daughter died. It seems likely that the children were stricken with meningitis, but the distracted family blamed it upon the foreign religion and the outraging of local spirits by a neighboring family.

"Curses of all the gods on Valiant One!" screamed her grandfather to the assembled neighborhood. "Curses, black curses, on the Chang family! Valiant One follows the foreign devils. The Chang family build a wall and anger the spirits. The spirits steal the lives of our beloved little ones. Curses! Curses! Curses!"

A missionary friend of the trembling little convert tried to quiet the storm, but the old man persisted.

"They build the wall. The spirits are angry. They carry off the souls of our children. The death of our children be on the Chang family! Let them bury them! They will have to bury them. What is more, they must buy fine, big caskets of the best wood, not small ones, but big ones, finely decorated. They must give the feast. Curse them!"

The missionary tried to reason. "The Changs are not responsible. This was some sudden sickness."

The old man would not listen. "The Changs *are* responsible. Were not the children well this morning? Are they not dead now? Who else could be the cause?" And the howling family and neighbors echoed the charges of the grandfather.

The missionary visited the Changs. They were miserably poor, and desperately frightened. Nobody had made any objection previously to their building a little mud wall. What were they to do? Two of them were Christians—which may have been the reason why the grandfather had so quickly perceived their guilt—and the others all seemed eager to follow any advice the foreigner might give. The missionary could only suggest that they do nothing and see if all did not turn out well.

It did not. That afternoon a Chang came frantically to the missionary.

"Oh, foreign teacher," he cried, "what are we to do now? The Fengs have put their dead children in our beds. We did not see them do it. Oh, we are lost! We have no money even for rice. How can we buy caskets and have a feast? How can we? How can we?"

"Appeal to the magistrate," suggested the missionary.

"No use; no use! The Fengs are related to a powerful outlaw, and even the official is afraid of the outlaws. Oh, they will tear down our house, break all our things, and kill us! Woe! Woe!"

The Changs bought the caskets and gave the feast. The Fengs forced them to the very limit of extravagance; they mortgaged themselves and all their little property for years to come. On the last day of the burial ceremonies the old grandfather, exhausted by his anger and the excitement, suddenly died, so that the tumult was loosed all over again. The life of the little Christian girl was only safe after she had been given work in a foreigner's home; the Changs are reduced to lifelong drudgery. All this as a result of the deaths of two children.

Against the extravagant outlays upon burials the new movement in China is setting all the force of its influence. To be sure, the reformers find the task difficult, for the popular verdict is likely to be that one who does not make a display at the death of a parent is lacking in filial piety. But there is so much common sense behind this reform that it is bound, in time, to win.

The New Tide of Thought does not reject utterly the custom that has been known in the West as ancestor worship. It sees much good accruing from a recognition of the link with the past. It rejects the idea of worship, but it suggests that a proper commemoration of the virtues of the dead may be of help in holding up the standards of character. With this view, Chinese Christians find much in common, and, while they refuse to go through any forms that might be mistaken for worship, they are more and more coming to methods of commemoration that will express the genius of their nation and still be recognized as Christian.

With the new age there have come to China many forms of social indulgence that give the leaders of the New Tide profound concern. Some of these, such as the prevalence of graft, are not new phenomena. But all of them seem in these days to be obtaining a power that makes them increasingly a menace to the public welfare. For this reason the reformers are trying to deal with gambling, grafting, drinking, and the social evil in the most courageous way. Not only are they working within the student bodies where, alas, much needs to be done along these lines, but they are trying to show the menace of these evils to the general public. In this, of course, they have the support of Christian bodies, and, in fact, many of the methods used have been devised by Christian agencies.

It must not be thought that the social reforms mentioned in this chapter have become universal throughout China. Some of them have barely begun to affect even the centers where the student influence is strongest. Social customs take a long time in the changing anywhere, and particularly in as conservative and massive a land as China.

But these changes are suggestive of the conditions that the New Tide has faced with its relentless "Why?" And it can be seen that, in attacking such evils as these, the New Tide is really going to the roots of China's difficulties. In the long run the wisdom of the new social modes should be sufficient to insure their adoption.

"Hold fast that which is good," said the apostle. The Chinese will always be ready to do that. But it is significant that, with the prestige of four thousand years of acceptance behind them, the reform leaders still insist that the social customs of China shall *prove* themselves good. There is more than hope for a land where that spirit lives. And, for Christians, there must be cheer in the realization that, as these issues come up for discussion, in practically every instance the leaders of the New Tide, although they may not call themselves Christians, are arriving at positions with which Christians are in accord.

Nor is this strange, for most of these social reforms have been advocated by Christians for years. The Christians may have been too few in numbers to bring such matters to the attention of much of the public, but at least their testimony has been clear. Now that reformers are coming from other sources, they must consider these Christian standards of social conduct. And the inevitable result has been that, as these honest leaders have studied these standards, they have acknowledged their value and have adopted them. So that it is possible to trace most of the changes that are coming among China's social customs directly back to Christian pioneering in the obscure years of the past. It was the Christian, after all, who first began to "prove all things."

V

CHINA'S NEW WOMEN

CHRISTIAN circles in Foochow had been stirred to their depths by a wedding. Out of the West, directly from years of study overseas, had come a young Chinese doctor to claim the favorite pupil in the mission girls' school as his bride. "A beautiful Christian home" was expected by everyone to result from the marriage.

The day after the wedding the missionary who had been almost a foster-mother to the girl was sitting in her office, going over in her mind the events of the previous day. How smoothly everything had gone! How sweet the bride had looked, with her embroidered scarlet dress and slippers! Surely it had been "a good job well done," and deserved a day of rest.

Suddenly the door burst open and in rushed the little bride.

"Dear teacher," she sobbed, "dear teacher, how can I stand it? How can I tell you? I am disgraced!"

"Disgraced! What do you mean?"

"My husband! He has disgraced me! I never want to see him again!"

Here was a strange outcome to the joyous festivities of the previous day! And it was a long time before the missionary had calmed her protégée enough to learn the details of the "disgrace" that her husband had brought upon her. But finally she discovered what had happened.

After the wedding, there had been a reception. And to the guests, who were speaking in English because of the presence of foreigners and Chinese from regions using different dialects, the doctor had introduced his bride as "my wife." So she had left him!

If this sounds like a mystery to you, so did it that afternoon to that missionary in Foochow. But the mystery cleared as the heart-broken bride stumbled ahead through the tale of her grief.

You see, the bride had learned her English in the mission school, where the Bible had been read with great thoroughness, both in Chinese and in English. And, insensibly, words in the English version came to have for her their literal value in the Chinese. As she read in English, her mind unconsciously supplied meanings from the parallel passages in Chinese.

Unfortunately for her, the Chinese version which thus formed her English dictionary was an early one, made by a missionary with a restricted knowledge of the new language, but a determination to pass the gospel into a new tongue without delay. And the only way in which that could be done was to have the missionary render the *meaning* of the passages in such colloquial Chinese as he could muster, and then trust a Chinese writer of the old school to turn that meaning into the *classical literary form* required by tradition. A procedure which, obviously, left the missionary largely at the mercy of the writer, and required a new translation before many years had passed. Yet the result was better than might have been expected.

So it was that the missionary and his collaborator did their task. And if you will examine the gospels, you will see that they could not go far in any one of them without running into that word that had caused so quick a tragedy in the new family—"wife." Naturally, that was not a word that gave the missionary-translator trouble. Nor did the brush of the old-style Chinese writer ever hesitate when it was dictated to him. Time after time, as it recurred, he put down two characters that for "ten thousand ages" had been used in the same connection.

Those were the two characters that popped into the mind of the girl in the mission school every time, in her English Bible, she read "wife." And those were the two characters that rose to torment her when her husband introduced her to his friends. And those two characters sent her back to her teacher with her heart broken but her jaw set. She would not live with a man who called her those two characters. For those two characters, literally translated, were "old horse"!

That bit of a sidelight on the difficulties of passing thought from one culture to another, which came so near to wrecking what is today one of the happiest homes in China, summarizes much of the ancient attitude of China toward her women. Dr. Ch'en Huan-chang, a brilliant American-educated exponent of Confucianism, has argued that, in the eyes of China's greatest sage, women stood on an equality with men, and that may be so. But the fact is that, both in law and in custom, China's women have for ages been treated as inferior to her men. In this China has not stood alone. There are still Christian nations in which the legal rights of women suffer in comparison with those of men. But in China too frequently social custom has operated even more disadvantageously, from the woman's standpoint, than law.

Woman has been at a disadvantage in the marital relation. To be sure, if it has been true that many women have not seen their mates until they met at the wedding altar, it has been equally true that the same number of husbands have blindly accepted the wives chosen by their families. Yet, taken from their own homes into families where custom has frequently seemed to demand severity upon the part of the elder members, many a young wife has felt that all she could do was to grit her teeth and bear her trials until the passing of years gave her a chance to rule over the wives of her sons.

In the letter of the law, divorce has always threatened the Chinese wife upon ridiculously easy terms. Any wife could be put away whose husband could complain of her barrenness, her unchastity, her disregard for her husband's parents, her talkativeness, her thieving, her bad temper, or her lack of good health. In practice, however, divorce has been, until recently, largely unknown. The practice of concubinage and plural marriage has entered into this situation.

Conditions in the homes have been anything but attractive, but Chinese women of the past have been rather rigidly held to their own hearths. Except in the mansions of the wealthy, there has been little attempt to secure comfort or beauty, and this, as has been pointed out in the investigation recently made of the city of Peking, has had much to do with driving men in the cities to the hectic amusements to be found elsewhere.

The extent to which many Chinese women have become drudges, without hope for relief, constantly amazes Westerners. In Hangchow recently a millworker fell under the attention of a missionary. Because of an incurable sickness, there were days when the pay this woman brought home from the mill was very small. And on these days she was always brutally beaten by her mother-in-law. It was clear that the woman could not much longer survive such treatment. Yet when a missionary sought a Chinese who might give competent advice, his interpretation concluded:

"The law does not make her stay with her cruel mother-in-law, but it does make her stay with her husband. If the husband is unwilling to leave his mother and set up a separate home, then his wife can only eat the bitterness. The husband can exhort his mother to treat his wife kindly, but the mother has power to command her son to do as she wishes, and he must treat her with respectful obedience."

For generations the Chinese have quoted this proverb: "A woman without talent is virtuous." That has represented to many the ideal for womanhood, the woman who knows that her place is in the home, or on the little farm-patch, living from one day to another without any interests beyond those immediately connected with the nourishment and clothing of her family.

However, in reporting these things that are true, it is easy to give an untruthful impression as to the actual conditions and position of the women of China. Even in the old China, woman's lot was a long way from being as hard as the West has sometimes believed it to have been. There is something in the experience of hundreds of centuries that accustoms one to conditions that, to a Westerner, might seem intolerable, so that they are never questioned. And again, it has happened that, by too much emphasis upon unusual cases, the situation as a whole has not been properly suggested.

The truth is that the unusual case could be employed to give a favorable impression of the position of Chinese women that would be as distorted as has been the old one. One might tell, for example, of that woman who began her career as an inconspicuous secondary wife from a minor branch of the Manchu household and ended it, only sixteen years ago, as the world-famous Empress Dowager. If you wish to read fascinating biography, try the life story of this woman, who, with the exception of Catherine of Russia, was probably the most powerful woman ruler that the world has ever known.

Nor is this example of a woman's achievement as unique in Chinese history as might be supposed. For of the 1,628 volumes in the Chinese biographical dictionary, 376 dealt with the lives of illustrious women. However much the law may have left her to her own resources, when one of these women has possessed initiative and personal force, she has been able to win a place of power in the same way that women have won such places in the West.

Let us not make the mistake of thinking of this power as reserved for women of the courts. In the homelier but more important realm of the ordinary family life, the Chinese woman has been far from being the poor tormented drab she has been pictured.

While living in the city of Nanking, our little family found it necessary, because of a shortage of missionary houses, to occupy a Chinese dwelling in a Chinese section. The houses were very flimsily built, and, in order to save material, the wall of our house was the wall of our neighbor's. Our neighbors heard everything that went on in our family, and we heard everything that went on in theirs. Mrs. Hutchinson, before the year was out, established quite a neighborhood reputation for herself as an unofficial arbitrator of family disputes. And in that intimate cross-section of Chinese life we found that there were at least as many homes where the woman was boss as there were where the man ruled!

Just behind us lived a farmer who cultivated a small truck-patch. He kept the affection of his wife by beating her regularly. Across the alley, in a thatched hut, dwelt a mighty ricksha-puller who gloried in the nickname of "Little Horse." He lived in abject terror of his wife. And when evening came there were husbands all around us who would slink off to the corner tea-house, while their wives stood bawling after them from the doorway, daring them to come home. Before we had lived under those conditions long, we discovered, as is the case in some Western communities, that the question as to whether or not the woman was a subservient slave in the house was largely a question of the personal factors involved.

The finger of scorn had sometimes been pointed at China because of the illiteracy of her women. No one has seen more clearly the weakness that the state has courted through this lack of education for its women than China's own reformers, who, in recent years, have opened all government schools on equal terms to women and men.

But, in a country where the margin of existence

is so narrow, and where the business of a woman is, first of all to rear a family, it can be seen that few women would have the opportunity for the twenty years of study necessary to obtain the old classical education.

China's women, however, are far from fools. That same close margin of existence that keeps them out of school forces them to sharpen their wits until, in the ceaseless bargaining that accompanies every Oriental transaction, they may be sure not to be worsted. There are many realms of knowledge that are totally unknown to the ordinary Chinese woman, but when it comes to the business of living, of keeping a household going, of providing that corrective advice without which any husband will occasionally make wrong choices, the women of China are as capable as those of any other part of the world.

Probably the most cruel misunderstanding current in the West has been that charging China's mothers with almost universal infanticide. We have told ourselves that human nature is much the same the world around, yet in this respect we have made ourselves believe that the women of China are not like others, and we have fallen victims to a legend of a land echoing with the cries of babies being tortured.

No one will say that girl babies have never been killed or sold in China. Both things have happened. They have happened in America, as we have had official and horrible evidence to prove. The press of poverty, and sometimes other motives, bring parents to the point where they will commit deeds for which there is no rational explanation. But to take these as normal pictures of the total womanhood of China is as false as it would be to take the results of the vice investigations made in certain American cities as normal pictures of the womanhood of America.

When our family was living in such enforced intimacy with the Chinese in Nanking, there were three babies in our home whom we loved, we thought, as much as it was possible for babies to be loved. Yet we found that we did not love our children a bit more than the parents all about us loved theirs. Indeed, to the Chinese it must have seemed that we did not love our children as well. For the Chinese child is generally despot of the household, while we did attempt to curb our youngsters occasionally.

Not only in respect to China and her women, but toward every country we, as Christians, need to apply one of the first corollaries of the Golden Rule: "Think of others as you would have others think of you."

Suppose a Chinese student in America should clip, during his four years of residence, every newspaper report of a murder, of a race riot, of a dope or liquor orgy, of a defiance of law such as burst out in the city of Omaha a few years ago when the city hall was burned and the mob tried to hang the mayor at a lamp-post. Suppose he should take that back

[93]

to China and present it as a picture of America. What a howl we should send up! Is it any wonder, then, that as the Chinese woman begins to learn how she has been regarded in Western lands, she is protesting that she has not been understood at all, but caricatured?

For even the meager basis of truth that lay behind all these misconceptions of China's women is passing. China's under-the-surface revolution is bringing forward a new type of womanhood. Soon the conception of Chinese women that dates back to reports twenty years old will be as out of date as a picture of American women would be that depicted them with the styles and the interests and ideas of the Civil War period.

If you were to board the Shanghai-Peking express train some day in September, it might easily chance that there would sit across the aisle a Chinese woman traveling alone. Her hair might be bobbed; she might be wearing the same sort of silk hosiery that is worn in the West; her eyebrows might be plucked; her cheeks rouged; her lips reddened. At her wrist she might be carrying a cigarette case. She might be returning home from a day at the races, where she had lost her wager on the favorite horse in the annual Grand Champions.

Such a picture is not very attractive, yet it is one that may be encountered in these changing days in China. It needs to be introduced here to strike a balance with the ideas of Chinese women that many have held. For it is possible to say that this woman is no more representative than the woman at the other extreme, and that, between the two, there is emerging a new type of Chinese woman who will play a large part in the nation's future.

The new type of Chinese woman is an eager student. When missionaries first opened schools for girls in China, they seemed to be facing the most impregnable opposition in the world. How many a devoted teacher of those days, as she planned how she might induce a handful of girls to enter her school, must have felt that the ramparts of conservatism were impregnable and could never be stormed? Today there do not begin to be enough schools to care for the thousands of Chinese girls who are seeking an education.

Government schools are now co-educational from the primary grades to the university. Mission schools have not yet carried the co-educational experiment, except in one or two cases, above the primary school. In some respects the mission schools are considered superior to those under governmental auspices, but the teaching in an institution like the National University at Peking or the Southeastern University at Nanking is not to be despised.

The courses offered women are substantially those followed in the schools and colleges of America. There are one or two special schools, such as the Normal School for Physical Education conducted by the Young Women's Christian Association, and the courses in home economics offered now in several places, that are preparing groups for forms of community service that will be of large value. The majority of the students follow what would generally be called a regular liberal arts course. To be sure, higher education can only be offered a small proportion of the girls who start the primary courses. But the costs involved do not permit more than a small proportion to seek such education.

Hundreds of Chinese girls have gone abroad to study. In the beginning, most of these were sent by the women's missionary societies, eager for a well-trained Chinese corps of workers. Today, girls are entering the competitive examinations that provide scholarships for overseas study, and others are going at their own expense. There are about two hundred Chinese girls at present studying in the schools of America.

The same spirit of independence that marks the boys is to be found in the girl students. Sometimes this leads to complications in school discipline. About half the students in one mission school for girls in Hangchow went on strike last year because the matron had been accused of striking one of the high school pupils. They secured rooms in the Lawyers' Association building, invited teachers from other schools to carry on their classes voluntarily, and then, with a large amount of public support, refused to return to their regular classes until the matron had been dismissed. It can be seen that this sort of spirit, while it grows out of a passion for justice and for freedom for the individual, has in it the seeds of much trouble.

A better sign of the independent spirit of China's new women students is to be found in the group of twenty who journeyed to Japan in 1923 to compete in the Far Eastern tennis championships. A few years ago such an adventure for Chinese girls would have been beyond the bounds of possibility. It shows the self-reliance of the new Chinese woman at its best.

These girl students have taken an active part in the Student Movement as it has sought to deal with China's political problems. Sometimes they have shown even a clearer insight and a more far-seeing vision than the agitators from the boys' schools. In 1919, for example, when the cry for the return of Tsingtau was raised, the girls from St. Mary's Hall, a mission school in Shanghai, issued this proclamation:

"Our first object is to help to build a greater China for the future. It is a big task and it is not a thing that we can accomplish in a day or two, but it is something that we have to try to do all through life. We must therefore be patient in our effort. It would be splendid to succeed in our demonstration about Tsingtau, but that alone would not be enough, for we want to do our part in building a strong China. This requires time, but if we, the people of the land, have true patriotism and develop it in the right way, a future righteous China is bound to come. In carrying out this aim we do not want to be too violent in our actions at one time and then let our patriotic feelings fade away as time goes on. If we are too excited now and try to do things that are beyond our capacity, we are harming rather than helping China, for such actions, unless they are wisely planned, may lead to lifelong regret, and that will not be true patriotism. Even though we lose Tsingtau temporarily, we can surely get it and all our lands back if our country is strong in time to come. So let us strive, not only for the present student demonstration, but also for a strong China."

Many a Chinese woman, however, cannot go to school. She may make a start, but before she has gone far the bony fingers of want stretch out to take her from the school-bench to the loom or the rice-field. Elsewhere we shall consider the part that industry is playing in the making of a new China. Here it is enough to say that at least eighty per cent of the thousands of operatives in the cotton and silk mills—the backbone of the new industry—are women and children, and that thirty-five per cent of all the workers in all forms of labor in the entire country are estimated by competent observers to fall into the same classification.

The woman and girl who leaves home before day-light to labor for twelve hours or more in the pulsing atmosphere of a modern machine-filled factory can never be the same kind of woman as the one who scarcely stirs outside her dooryard from week-end to week-end. And the instant a woman begins to be paid, however poorly, in cash rather than in food and clothing and shelter, she is sure to assume a different attitude toward any position in her community.

Women are entering many lines of industry, not only as laborers, but as leaders. One Chinese woman covered the Paris Peace Conference as a reporter for certain Canton newspapers. There are said to be more than forty factories in Canton owned and operated by women. A woman is clerk of the Cantonese parliament, and edits the "Parliamentary Record." On the Canton-Shamshui railway women act as secretaries, ticket collectors, and inspectors. Leave progressive Canton, and in Shanghai you find a woman as manager of the Ladies' Savings Department of the Shanghai Commercial and Savings Bank. You will find a group of women promoting a woman's bank in Peking. Make your way far inland to Nanchang, capital of the province of Kiangsi, and you find a woman owning and operating the city's electric light and telephone plants.

In professional life Chinese women are coming more and more to the fore. Teaching, nursing, and medicine are the callings that make the most appeal, although there are many other lines in which women are finding a place. More attention has probably been given to the women doctors of China than to any other of the new type of Chinese women. For years the work of women like Dr. Mary Stone, now of Shanghai, or Dr. Li Bi Cui, of a city far in the interior of Fukien province, has been known throughout China and elsewhere. A conspicuous member of the same group has been Dr. Ida Kahn, a classmate of Dr. Stone's at the University of Michigan, and the head of a great hospital in Nanchang.

Dr. Kahn is one of those dynamic women who seem to have time to do anything. Not only does she run a large hospital, but she has taken a vigorous part in Chinese reform movements, has written for English and Chinese periodicals, and has frequently turned in to clean up some of the dark spots in her own city. When funds for her hospital ran out, she took work in a government institution until she had received enough to put the Nanchang hospital back on its feet. When she wants something done, and done quickly, she summons the provincial officials, who come without delay, and agree without delay to do whatever she asks. She is a positive, uncompromising person, who gets things done. Certain famous women who might be named from past history must have been much the same.

China's new women have given themselves unsparingly to all sorts of reform movements. They have led in the agitation against foot-binding. They have fought the opium evil relentlessly. They have organized a Woman's Christian Temperance Union, with Chinese officers, and are agitating against the slowly growing liquor evil. They will undertake without misgiving great campaigns, in centers like Peking, to teach the masses how to have hygienic home conditions, with demonstration centers in which totally illiterate women can be shown what their homes should be. In the movements toward reform in the industrial realm it has not been accidental that the Young Women's Christian Association should have taken a leading part.

During the winter of 1922-23 the girls in that remarkable Christian school, Ginling College, Nanking, were studying the application of Christianity to social conditions. Soon they began to show signs of restlessness, which culminated in the decision that the theories learned in the classroom should be put into immediate practice. Accordingly, negotiations were entered into with the ricksha-pullers of the city, as a result of which a scale of rates was worked out which was accepted by the men as fair. This scale has been made public throughout Nanking, and serves to protect one of the most pitiful groups of toilers of that city.

Within the last year or two what might be called China's feminist movement has begun to take concrete form. Soon after the revolution of 1911 there were sporadic outbreaks in favor of equal suffrage, but nothing permanent appeared at that time. Now, however, there are associations for the securing of suffrage and of equal rights in ten provinces.

The Woman Suffrage Association has announced this platform:

[101]

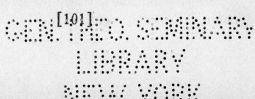

1. For the purpose of protecting woman's rights, all the articles in the constitution partial to men should be abolished.

2. In order to secure economic independence for women, the limiting of inheritance rights to men should be abolished.

3. In demanding equality of opportunity in education, the old system of giving women a limited education adapted only to domestic affairs should be abolished.

The Woman's Rights League calls for these things:

1. All educational institutions shall be open to women.

2. Women shall have the same constitutional rights as men.

3. The relation between man and wife, parents and children, rights of inheritance, property and conduct laws shall be based upon the principle of equality.

4. Marriage laws based upon equality between men and women shall be enacted.

5. For the protection of girls the "age of consent" shall be incorporated in the criminal law, and a law shall be enacted whereby the taking of concubines shall be considered as bigamy.

6. Licensed prostitution, the slave trade, and foot-binding shall be prohibited.

7. Protective labor legislation based upon the principle of "equal pay for equal work" and "protection of motherhood" shall be enacted.

Many forms of feminism are being agitated in the growing number of papers that cater to the women of China. Two years ago the citizens of Tientsin and Peking were roused when they read this advertisement in one of the daily papers:

"In view of the national chaos and social disorder, it is necessary for a modern Chinese girl to

acquire the highest education possible in order to be able to face the problem of life with full equipment. As for me, my education has been rather limited and my desire to prosecute further studies is above the boiling point. Several times I have asked my father to grant my wish. Unfortunately, my parents are so conservative that they have declined to consider my request favorably. Under these circumstances I cannot but leave my dear ones in order to realize my ambitious aim. From December 3, 1921, I have severed all my connection with my family."

The new-style editor saw a chance for a feature in this advertisement and invited the opinions of readers as to whether or not the girl had been justified in publishing such a manifesto. A flood of letters poured in, so strongly in favor of the girl that at last her father, a well-known scholar of the old school, agreed to compromise, using the editor as mediator. The treaty of peace, as finally published, contained these stipulations:

1. The parents promised to support the girl and her sister in school.

2. In case the girls felt it wise to go to a boarding-school, the parents promised to make no objections.

3. The daughters were to be free to choose their own courses of study.

4. The daughters were to be allowed to buy and read any decent books, magazines, and newspapers.

5. The daughters were to have freedom of correspondence, but were to report their movements to their parents.

6. The parents were to promise to support their daughters in case they wished to study abroad.

7. The girls were not to be betrothed before the age of twenty-five. If they should then have their own views on matrimony, they were to be free to lay them before their parents. There should be no betrothal without consent of the girls.

Here, in a newspaper advertisement and its aftermath, is something of a sketch of new China's new woman. Where has she come from? She is, of course, a part of this inner revolution that is remaking so much of Chinese life. But she has antecedents of her own.

China's history contains scattered stories of several women who achieved careers for themselves, notably the great soldier, Mu-lan. But it is probable that the emancipation of China's women had a religious origin when first Buddhist convents were set up, and hundreds of devotees broke family ties to enter sanctuaries. However, the life of a Buddhist nun is largely a life of segregation and abstinence. It was in Christian religious work that the woman of China found her first real opportunity for active freedom.

No sooner did women as missionaries bring their living object-lesson to the East than they found it necessary to secure Chinese women as their helpers. These in many cases had to fight the battle for women's rights before they could enter upon their service. The old-fashioned Bible woman, with her cheap clothes, her lack of education, and her limited outlook, may not have seemed to some a romantic figure, but she was the pioneer in whose footsteps walk all the emancipated women of modern China.

Chinese women still look overseas for inspiration in their struggle toward a new day. Not long ago a Chinese, Mrs. H. C. Mei, was addressing a meeting in Shanghai, telling of the changed outlook of the women of her country.

"It is not flattery to say that Chinese women look for feminist ideals and inspiration from America," she said. "From American missionaries Chinese girls first imbibed the sense of human personality which their men-folk for ages past had all but denied them. From American schools they learned the comforting strength of an independent mind and the sweetness of real freedom; from American homes they drank in the wholesome atmosphere of domestic harmony with which they are making normal the Chinese household; from the high-spirited and achieving American women they have received the lesson of self-respecting and self-reliant character, whether it be in taking up a professional career, or entering the ranks of bread-winners, or home-building."

Of course, all the two hundred million women of China are not like the women spoken of in this chapter. But the number is increasing, and the day is on the way when the whole vast lump will be leavened.

VI

BENEATH THE SMOKESTACKS

It was about half-past three on one of those cold, damp mornings that Shanghai knows so well in early spring. The missionary rolled over again in bed, digging his ears down into the pillows, trying to escape the cries from outside his window. He knew only too well what the wailings meant, for he had heard many like them before. Some child was being driven to work in a factory against her will. Soon she would be gone, and then sleep would be possible. And, anyway, what could the missionary possibly do by interfering?

"Let me die; kill me if you like; I won't go!" came in screams through the window, followed by the thud of belaboring hands, more groans, and the shrill curses of a woman.

Finally, the missionary could stand it no longer. Slipping into a robe, he hurried down to the back gate. It was still so dark that he had to be guided by the sounds, and when he reached the source of all the commotion he had to touch the arm of the woman before she realized that anyone was near.

The child, a little girl who did not look more than eight, but who was probably nearer ten, was lying on the wet, muddy cobbles, moaning hysterically. Suddenly she discovered that someone else was near —a foreigner. She had heard stories of the dreadful things these red-haired beings did to little girls, and before the woman could put a detaining hand on her, she had vanished in the dark.

The woman, evidently a country woman from north of the river, with a face that was not unpleasant in spite of the job that she had just been engaged in, started to follow, but the missionary demanded that she stay. Her feet were bare, and she wore nothing but a loose jacket and short trousers. Although it was a cold night, her face was streaming with perspiration from her recent efforts.

"Is it necessary to punish the child like that?" the missionary asked.

"Yes; she won't go to work."

"But isn't she too young to work, especially at this time of the night? Where is her father?"

"She has none."

"Then can't you support her yourself? Surely you know it is bad for her to work in a factory at this age."

"I can't support her and myself, too."

"How much do you get?"

"Twenty cents small money (about ten cents in American currency), and with the price of rice what it is now, that is hardly enough to feed one mouth."

"How much does the girl get?"

"Ten cents. With what we both earn, we have barely enough to eat. If she loses a day, we go hungry."

"What time do you have to be at the factory?"

"Four o'clock, and leave about seven in the evening."

"You mean that that child has to work fifteen hours a day?"

"Yes, about that."

"Where do you live?"

"Over there," and she waved toward the village of mud and thatched huts, a stone's throw distant, many of them not high enough for a man to stand upright in, and most of them consisting of a single small room. Only a couple of months before this whole little settlement had burned. But in three days' time it had been rebuilt.

"Where do you work?"

"In a cigarette factory over there," and the woman pointed in the opposite direction.

"What is the name of the factory?"

"I don't know."

"Well, if you will wait for me here while I get dressed, I will pay your wages for the day, for I want to find out more about this factory where you work."

But when the missionary returned, the woman had lost courage and disappeared.

And that is only one case of thousands more or less similar, though fortunately there are really not many mills in China that run one shift from fifteen to sixteen hours a day. But the plight of the little girl, brought from her home on the farm-lands north of the Yangtze to a cigarette factory in the great city, is symptomatic of the shift that is, with gathering force, beginning to affect all China's people.

For more than forty centuries most of China's people have been farmers. And what fine farmers they have been! On their little plots of land, seldom more than a third of an acre in size, they have raised three and four crops a year in rotation for thousands of years. Such an authority as Professor King, of the University of Wisconsin, tells us that they have produced the highest yield per acre of any farmers in the world. We Westerners, under whose hands rich land is often exhausted after a century, should ponder these facts before we begin to look down upon the Chinese farmer, despite his use of primitive tools.

China is still predominantly agricultural, and will so remain for a century to come. It is estimated that eighty-five per cent of her people are still farmers, and when you speak of Chinese industry, you must always have these sturdy men of the soil in mind. That is why so much of the most effective missionary work today deals with the aiding of the farmers.

But the shift from the land to the machine, from the country to the city, has begun, and it will hardly cease until China, with her enormous resources, has become one of the great manufacturing nations. Just how many Chinese are now engaged in factory industry it is impossible to estimate. In the city of Shanghai, the industrial capital, there are about 550,000 workers, and the numbers in the rest of the country would probably bring the total above the two-million mark. More impressive than any such figures is the growth of whole industrial cities.

Shanghai is a case in point. We have grown accustomed to thinking of Shanghai, with its population of more than a million, as one of the world's great cities. A recent writer has said that, with its situation at the mouth of the world's most populous watershed, Shanghai is bound to become the largest city on the globe. Many Americans, with all their worship of speed, hardly realize that the growth of Shanghai has been as remarkable as that of Chicago. When the first settlers built their fort at what is now Chicago, they were a few years ahead of the first traders who settled near the wretched little fishing village that was then Shanghai. But modern industry, as it has made its slow progress in China, has forced the population of this city, located where the great river flows into the sea, ever upward. And now that the industrial development is on in earnest, the city is expanding like a caliph's dream.

Should a traveler who was last in China a decade ago make the night trip by rail from Shanghai to Nanking today, he might rub his eyes as the train stopped in a station a few miles west of Soochow. For beyond the station he would see the most modern type of street lights illuminating the roadway, and beyond there would rise, story upon story, the yellow squares of factory windows. Ten years ago a self-respecting train would scarcely deign to whistle as it rushed through the little village here; today the traveler would be looking upon the great industrial city of Wusih.

Or the same traveler might open a paper and see there an advertisement written in the same sort of language that would be employed by an American booster club: "Come to Nantungchow, China's model city!" And if the appeal proved strong enough to take him up the river to the place where a former high official, Mr. Chang Chien, has brought reality to his dreams, he would find a widespreading municipality, with broad streets, fine buildings, and varied industries, illustrating the possibilities of a new kind of prosperity to all the lower Yangtze valley.

"When I first came to Tsinan," a resident of the capital of Shantung Province said not long ago, "the only factory chimney in the city was that of the German-built electric-light plant. Now there are more than thirty stacks belching forth soot."

A recent estimate puts the number of modern factories in China at fourteen hundred, and there are thousands more of a semi-modern type. Besides these, there are the innumerable places, often no better than hovels, where some of China's most characteristic products are manufactured.

In Nanking, for example, there are whole streets

given over to the weaving of silks and satins. The looms are set up in courtyards and rooms of the little houses. Late at night you may hear their wooden clacking, and I never was able to get up before that noise had started in the morning. The rooms are very dark. They have dirt floors. Children, dogs, and sometimes a pig or so, wander about. But in some way these weavers manage to produce bolts of the most delicate pink and green and blue silks, with exquisite designs woven into them, and without the semblance of a spot appearing.

The commercial attaché of the United States in China has reported that the Westernized industries of the country already include cotton-mills, silk-mills, oil-mills, woolen-mills, sawmills, paper-mills, flour-mills, ship-building works, knitting works, steel works, printing works, smelting-works, water works, glass works, brick works, canneries, net factories, match factories, railway shops, sugar factories, cigarette factories, newspapers, egg-drying factories, furniture factories, chinaware and porcelain factories, distilleries, breweries, arsenals, and numberless smaller manufacturing enterprises. The cotton- and silk-mills form the backbone of the new industrial order. Some sense of the rate of growth may be caught from the knowledge that, between 1919 and 1922, the number of cotton-mills jumped from 49 to 102. Forty-six per cent of these are owned by foreign capital.

This rapid growth of a Westernized industry has

led to an increase of more than six hundred per cent in the imports and exports of China since the opening of this century! No wonder that other nations, eager to secure wealth for their people by the control of world markets, see in China a great prize to be grasped at almost any price.

Much of the industry that is growing up in the East today is a direct importation from the West. This is, of course, true of all the factories that depend upon power looms or similar machinery. It is frequently true of other forms of labor that, on the surface, appear indigenous. The ricksha-puller, for instance, is in a form of work that takes a hideous toll of human life. We are likely to think of the ricksha as distinctively Oriental. But the truth is that the two-wheeled, man-pulled buggy was invented by a missionary who found wheelbarrows too slow a method of transportation.

Silk weaving was one of the great industries of China two thousand years ago. We still think of it as distinctly Chinese, and so it is. But a few years ago it appeared that China's silk industry must disappear before the competition of the silkworms of Japan and other countries. The industry is not yet back to its proper place, but it is making long strides toward recovery. And this largely because mission schools, notably the University of Nanking, working in cooperation with the Department of Agriculture of the United States, have stepped in to determine scientifically what has been the matter with China's silkworms, and to produce a breed that would meet the competition of the rest of the world.

Much the same thing has been done by the same school to make possible the cultivation of cotton. The profitable production of the raw materials upon which China's most rapidly developing industries depend, therefore, is due to the contribution of the West through the mission school.

Yet the growth of a new industry has not been wholly the result of Western initiative. In speaking before the Bankers' Club in New York City a few years ago, Mr. B. L. Putnam Weale, the British writer, told of the metamorphosis that had come to a shop located within a stone's throw of his home in Peking. The story epitomizes the way in which Chinese are entering into new fields of industry. Until three or four years ago this shop confined its attention to the repair of pots and kettles. One day a Ford that had been in collision with a telegraph post was brought to the shop for minor repairs and, out of the success of that adventure, an automobile garage blossomed forth. Not more than a year later a big English steam-roller panted up to the door in the last stages of exhaustion. The proprietor and his employees devoted a day to studying the monster. At the end of that time they went to work and, with cold chisel and main strength, removed the boiler and most of the interior parts of the roller. For forty-eight days the work never stopped by day or night. Before it was finished, practically all of the community had borne a hand in it. But, at the end of that time, the steam-roller, repaired and repainted, lumbered off in triumph. The old pot and kettle shop had climbed one rung higher.

If you will let your imagination play with an incident like this for a few minutes, and then remember that, in similar ways, it can be multiplied hundreds of times in other parts of China, you will see that, in this under-the-surface change of which we have been talking, this industrial shift may prove as important as any other part of China's real revolution.

When the United States entered the nineteenth century it was ninety per cent agricultural. In 1910 only thirty-three per cent of its people lived on the farm. When China entered the twentieth century it was ninety per cent agricultural. If a shift from the farm to the factory involving only a third of these takes place during the century (a conservative forecast), more than the entire present population of the United States will be affected.

When, at the beginning of the last century, England made the shift from the land to the machine, it brought years of disorder from which it seemed at times as though international anarchy might result. If that were true in conservative and constricted England, with the difficult communications of that day, what will be the effect of such a shift on the part of China's vast and undisciplined masses?

Can you change the industrial order in terms of continents without having continental upheavals?

The answer to that question largely depends, of course, upon the manner in which the change takes place. And it is here that the situation in a country like China should cause the most grave alarm. It is too easy for the superficial traveler, because he sees the black smoke belching from the factory chimneys of these cities of the East, to go home and assure the Kiwanis Club or the Rotary Club or the Chamber of Commerce that "these heathen nations are actually being civilized, by George!" But there is more involved here than the smoke in the chimney or the product in the packing-room, or the rise in imports and exports. There is a great human problem and a great moral problem, with an actual menace to future world unity. At the foot of the smokestacks of China the Christian may find a tremendous challenge to his faith.

For what kind of labor is it that tends the machines in these new industrial centers of the Orient? What sort of wages are being paid these people as they desert the little farm-holdings that have nurtured their ancestors for centuries? Under what conditions are these recruits to the machine forced to work? Will this industry eventually bless or curse?

Mr. Sherwood Eddy was in China in 1923, and renders vivid testimony to conditions as he saw them.

"One of the first plants visited in a leading industrial center was a match factory, which is said to be the best of its kind in that city," he says. "We found there eleven hundred employees, for the most part boys from nine to fifteen years of age, working from 4 A.M. to 8:30 P.M., with a few minutes of intermission at noon. They work on an average fifteen hours a day, seven days a week, with no Sunday of rest. The boys receive from six to ten cents, and the men about twenty-five cents a day. The poisonous fumes of phosphorus and sulphur and the dust from the other chemicals burned our lungs even in the short half hour we were in the factory. Eighty men and boys in this plant have to visit the hospital each day for treatment. Many suffer from 'phossy jaw,' where the bones of the face decay on account of the cheap grade of phosphorus. This could be avoided if somewhat more expensive chemicals were used, but it would cut down the profits, which are said to be very high.

"We next visited a Chinese rug factory making the most beautiful 'Persian' rugs for use in the homes of millionaires in America and Europe. But who are making these rugs? Twelve hundred boys and young men, from nine to twenty-five years of age, are here employed. The foremen receive $8, while other men average $4.50 a month and their food. Men and boys are working on an average of sixteen hours a day, from 5:30 A.M to 10 P.M.

The majority of the boys serve as apprentices for a period of three years and receive *no pay whatever* but only get their food. This 'apprenticeship' is only a blind alley. After the boys serve three years there is no future for them in the business.[1] When they are graduated from their apprenticeship, they can become ricksha coolies and earn on an average fifteen cents a day. The fifty thousand ricksha pullers in Peking average less than this amount. After five years of this work they are usually broken in health and are then useless. The ricksha coolie who brought me home last night was endeavoring to support a family of four upon his small earnings. If he has no work for a day, he must go without food.

"The third plant visited was a Chinese tannery run by a Christian. The conditions here are said to be the best of all the smaller factories in the city. The usual sixteen hours' work a day is reduced by this Christian to ten. Men and boys earn from $5.50 to $8.50 a month. Apprentices sleep in a loft above the shop, and in addition to their food and clothes, receive thirty-five cents a month during the first year. The second year they are paid a dollar a month, and the third year nearly four dollars a month or thirteen cents a day. The industrial department of the Y.M.C.A. is permitted to put on a program of welfare work, athletics, and games for the workers. It was most touching to see the faces of these boys light up with gratitude when they saw

[1] This is so because the factory proprietor hires more apprentices to take the places of those to whom wages would have to be paid.—P. H.

[118]

FORTY PER CENT OF THE WORKERS IN THE COTTON AND SILK MILLS OF SHANGHAI ARE CHILDREN.

WHERE EAST AND WEST MEET ON THE HANKOW WATER-FRONT.

the industrial secretary of the Y.M.C.A. enter the shop. He knows them personally and is bringing a ray of light into the hearts of hundreds of these weary little toilers.

"The fourth factory was a Chinese weaving establishment making cloth upon primitive looms. At present there are 15,000 boys in the city working on these looms. In normal times there are 25,000 employed, but many are now out of work. The wages paid to the men average $4.50 a month, or about fifteen cents a day. The workers average about eighteen hours a day, from 5 A.M. to 11 P.M, working seven days a week. The majority of the boys are apprentices who receive no wage whatever, but only their food."

Equally grim are the reports from other industries. A friend of mine visited the Pinghsiang colliery in Kiangsi Province last year. After some hesitation the manager allowed him to go with one shift of miners two miles underground, where he found men, stark naked, streaming with sweat, picking away at the open coal seam. From this suffocating gallery the men were carried back to the cold air of the upper levels at 4:30 o'clock in the morning.

All things considered, the conditions in this mine were superior to those to be found in many similar industries in China. Yet the men felt that they were being crushed by an inexorable industrial machine. As the driver of the engine that was to carry the little party to the surface took a Bible, he said:

[119]

"Sir, you are bringing us the Christian gospel, which is very good. But, sir, the condition of the men in the mines is very bitter."

"It is better since you struck, isn't it?"

"Yes, they have quit beating the men, but we work long hours and get small pay."

"Don't you get thirty cents a day and your board and lodging?"

"No," replied the engine-driver. "My pay is now twenty-eight cents. I get one meal from the company, but I have my family here and rent my own house. Some of the men get less and work more. These men you have just seen digging will work until 4.30 tomorrow morning. They get one meal served them in here, eat when they go out and just before they come in. They are fed and housed by the company, which pays them besides fifteen cents a day. Some really work as much as fifteen hours; and when you add an hour for meals and eight for sleep, there is nothing else in life. Even on a twelve-hour shift one has little time or energy left.

"Most of us have been here many years. I came soon after the mines opened. Very few new toilers have come in recent years. Three thousand men are toiling at these underground tasks, and our lot is bitter and hopeless. Twice a month we have a rest day, but we often lose that by a change of shifts, when the day workers change with the night workers. You see why we can't often go to the church where they preach the good gospel you bring."

It is in the mills that laboring conditions are to be seen at their worst. In fact, so bad are these conditions that in many of the mills they cannot be seen. Strict orders have debarred outsiders from passing the gates, so that there can be no first-hand report of the way in which thousands of mere children have to stand through the long nights, slaves of the great machines.

Yet if you will take your stand in Yangtsepoo Road in Shanghai shortly before half-past five any evening, you will see what sort of human material it is that is being fed into this new industrial order. At your back, stretching from the street to the river bank, are the great mills, many of them concrete-and-steel structures. Across the road are countless Chinese shops and tea-houses. Up and down the street clatter tram-cars and automobiles. Rickshas jog by. And in and out of this ceaseless traffic weave long lines of wheelbarrows, each barrow freighted with the workers who are to go on duty at 5:30 and remain there until the same time to-morrow morning.

I have never seen one of these wheelbarrows that bore fewer than six workers at that time of day. Eight is more common, and ten might be called the standard load. Every so often a barrow will pass bearing workers so young that fourteen of them can be wheeled by a single coolie.

That is the sort of a foundation upon which men, in their desire for quick and high profits, are trying to build China's new industrial life. It has been stated that, taking into consideration all the industries in modern China, including those that must use nothing but mature male labor, the workers are fifteen per cent women and twenty per cent children under fourteen years of age! And a careful investigation of the cotton- and silk-mills of Shanghai disclosed the fact that forty per cent of the workers are women and forty per cent children.

A group of interested Christians tried to give a Christmas party to these silk-mill girls of Shanghai a few years ago. One hundred and twenty of them came—one hundred and twenty morsels of dismal humanity. Most of them had bound feet, and the tips of their fingers were white from constant dipping into the hot water in which the cocoons are handled. These children ranged from six to twelve years of age, and were probably familiar with the mills from their earliest days, for mothers frequently bring their babies and place them among the piles of cocoons between feedings. Then when the child is old enough, it is taught to sort the cocoons and pull off the waste, and so it spends the long days, sitting on a little stool in the dark, dusty, unheated room, picking endlessly away.

The youngsters at this Christmas party were curious as to what was in store for them. But the best efforts of the most accomplished recreational leaders of the city could do nothing to arouse them. They had been utterly beaten down by the monotony of the factory. Their young strength had been mortgaged even before they were born.

Even after they have been worked thus hard, these mill-hands frequently receive only a pittance. Wages have been slowly forced up in China since the close of the World War (as in other countries, they have not kept pace with the rise in living costs), but still today, in the most highly paid labor center in China, Shanghai, skilled women workers in the silk-mills receive but from thirty-six to forty cents a day, gold; unskilled women workers but from twenty-eight to thirty-five cents a day; and girls but from fifteen to twenty cents a day. And it is estimated that more than seventy per cent of all the workers in the country are working the seven-day week.

This exploitation is reaching out from the mills to cast its blight upon the homes around the mills. A system of sweatshop labor is coming into existence that bids fair to go far toward the undermining of Chinese village life.

A group of Christians wanted to establish a school for the children of workers. Having secured a location and a teacher, they set out to gather a constituency. They went to a little group of shacks near a factory center, expecting to find the children eager to attend the new school while their parents were at work. The children were eager enough, but not many of them could enrol in the school. For these were the conditions in the eight houses that made up that little village:

[123]

In the first there was only one boy. He was thirteen years old and worked in an iron-foundry.

In the second, two little girls and a woman were found making match-boxes. Each girl made two thousand a day, and the woman from four to five thousand. They were paid four cents (American money) for every thousand boxes finished.

In the third house they were told that the three girls, seven and eight years old, began work in a thread factory at 6 A.M. daily. They worked twelve hours and earned from ten to fifteen cents a day.

In the fourth house the children were making a thousand match-boxes a day.

In the fifth house a boy of seven and a girl of fourteen were working in the thread factory. Their top limit of pay was twenty cents a day.

In the sixth house there were two girls, each five years old. But they could not go to school, for they were learning a trade. They received no pay during their apprenticeship.

In the seventh house a seventeen-year-old girl was making five thousand matches in a twelve-hour day.

In the eighth house there was a girl who worked in a cigarette factory, packing boxes. Her wages were a cent for every fifty boxes packed. In the same factory she said that boys and girls five and six years of age were working a twelve-hour day. A third of the force was working eighteen hours.

Naturally, an industry conducted under such conditions expects to pile up enormous profits. To our shame be it said that many of the worst offenders have been companies formed by investors from Christian lands. The condition of one of these companies was thus reported in a trade journal:

"The profits of the —— factory again surpass $1,000,000. To those who bestow thought on the progress of textile industries in China, the following particulars concerning this concern may be of interest. The company was started in 1904 with a paid-up capital of $600,000, divided into 6,000 shares of $100 each. The capital was increased to $900,000 in 1916. . . . For the past two years it has been running night and day without intermission. . . . The working hours are from 5:30 A.M. to 5:30 P.M., and from 5:30 P.M. to 5:30 A.M., respectively. No meals are supplied by the factory. Most of the cotton is produced locally. . . . It will be seen that the company is in an exceptionally favorable position. With the raw product at its door, an abundant and absurdly cheap labor supply to draw on, and no vexatious factory laws to observe, it is not surprising that its annual profits should have exceeded its total capital on at least three occasions."

No, it is not surprising. Neither is it surprising that even the Chinese, tormented by hunger as they are, are beginning to rebel against such ruthless exploitation. A labor movement has sprung into being within the last few months that is putting a new complexion on the industrial situation in China. For centuries China has had her guilds. But these have been nothing more than associations of employers. Now she has her labor-unions of employees, and already they are showing power.

It was in the spring of 1922 that the laboring man first began to realize his own strength in China. Sailors on foreign-owned ships struck in the harbor of Hongkong. For a time the companies laughed at the threat, thinking it would be easy to fill the vacant places. But one ship after another was tied at anchor until there were finally more than 250,000 tons of shipping lying idle. At last the shipping companies gave in.

The effect was immediate up and down the China coast. Labor-unions came into being in all the port cities. In Shanghai, for example, more than sixty such unions were formed within a month after the close of the Hongkong strike. These embraced all sorts of crafts. In Canton and Chaochow, one of its main suburbs, there were more than fifty strikes within the next nine months, and nine tenths of them, because of public support, were successful. It is even reported that as far inland as the province of Hunan, when the soldiers attempted to run trains on the northern section of the Canton-Wuchang railway, strikers threw their bodies on the tracks until more than a hundred had been killed or injured, thus bringing the railway to an effective standstill.

The springing up of this labor movement, with

the publication of drastic lists of demands, moved the Ministry of Agriculture and Commerce, early in 1923, to promulgate a list of regulations for the control of factory labor. To be sure, these regulations are only on paper, and will never be enforced by the present feeble government. But there is some value in having them on paper, as a recognized standard toward which to work.

There are twenty-eight articles in the list of government labor regulations. The employment of boys under the age of ten and of girls under twelve is forbidden. Child labor is defined as that done by boys of less than seventeen and girls less than eighteen, and is not to exceed eight hours a day. Adult labor is not to exceed ten hours a day. There shall be no child labor at night. Educational facilities are to be offered all workers, especially children, and there is provision for care and compensation for injured and sick workers. Women are to be adequately cared for before, during, and after childbirth.

It takes no prophet to see that the industrial situation as it has been developing up to this time in China has been leading toward the same sort of economic warfare as the West has known. The pursuit of profits at whatever cost in human life has been making the workers more and more bitter, and the organization of labor-unions has been but the first step in an endless class warfare. Were there no other elements in the situation than those already mentioned, the industrial side of China's inner change would be as bitter and exhausting an affair as any of the industrial disputes that have tormented England and America.

Fortunately, the Christian forces have swung into action in this field in a way that gives a promise of better days in the near future. Warned by the experience of the West, the Church has been able to point out the need for industrial justice if there is to be any peace within the nation. The contribution of the Church really began to make itself felt a few years ago when Miss Zung Wei Tsung, a secretary of the Young Women's Christian Association, began to conduct a column in the leading Chinese daily of Shanghai, setting forth conditions in the mills of that city. It was the first time that the situation had been forced upon the attention of the city in a way that could not be avoided.

The gathering of six hundred students from thirty-seven nations in the convention of the World's Student Christian Federation at Peking, early in 1922, gave the movement a further impetus. For these students laid down as their creed, "The construction of our ideal society is based on the spirit and teachings of Jesus Christ, and we therefore believe in:

1. The absolute sacred value of the individual.

2. Love as the basis of human fellowship.

3. Mutual service as the means of human progress."

And these students then went ahead to present a program for industrial democracy that struck hard at the sort of abuses that are rampant in China.

It remained for the National Christian Conference of 1922 to bring the matter to head. Here 1,189 delegates, representing all parts of the Church in China, picked this as one of the two subjects for action by the entire conference—regulation of the opium traffic was the other—and, with but one dissenting voice, adopted a progressive industrial policy as the embodiment of Christian ideals, and called for the immediate acceptance by all industries of three rules:

1. No employment of children under twelve years of age.

2. One day's rest in seven.

3. The safeguarding of the health of the worker through the limitation of working hours, improvement of working conditions, and installation of safety devices.

In the time that has passed since this standard was adopted, the Christians have gone about organizing groups in almost all China's industrial centers that will press to see it put into practice. In two important cities, Peking and Cheefoo, the Chinese Chambers of Commerce have been induced to adopt the Christian standard. (The victory in Cheefoo may be of peculiar interest to some American ladies, for it is there that most of the world's hair-nets are manufactured.) Advance legislation has been passed in Hongkong. The regulations of the government have already been mentioned.

And what does it all mean? Surely it means that China is facing an entirely new sort of life. With her immense resources, both in man-power and in the raw materials that the world so needs, she is bound to become, within a century, one of the great manufacturing nations. This change has already begun, and in a manner to warn of trouble not far off. But some have seen the warnings, and a bettering of laboring conditions is already apparent. One great agency for this improvement is the Christian Church. In fact, to many grateful Chinese the Church seems to have been the agency that has sounded the alarm and pointed to a safer path of development. To the workers of the new China, therefore, the Church can speak with an authority beyond that known in many other lands.

VII

THE STRUGGLE FOR FAITH

Two students who had studied in America were walking away from the service conducted for English-speaking Chinese on Sunday afternoons in the Y.M.C.A. at Shanghai.

"I haven't seen you here for some time, Mr. Tang," one greeted the other.

"No, Dr. Lo; for this is the first time I have been at the meeting for a good many months."

"Have you been out of town?"

"No, I'm in business here. The truth is that I have rather lost interest in this sort of thing."

"I'm sorry to hear you say that. I had understood that you were active in Christian work."

"There was a time," Mr. Tang said slowly, "when I was active. You know that I was educated in a mission school. While there, I acted as one of the officers of the student Y.M.C.A. Then I won a scholarship for study abroad, which gave me three years of postgraduate work in America.

"During my first year in America I attended the usual religious services at college. I was too busy trying to find my place in the unfamiliar life of an American campus to go outside much. And, in the rush of classes, questions connected with religion hardly entered my mind.

"Then came my first vacation period, when I

started out to see some of the actual processes of American industry. I lived in four American cities that summer, and I had some unpleasant experiences while hunting lodgings and in other ways, I can tell you."

"Yes, I know what you mean," answered Dr. Lo, quietly.

"There's not much Christian brotherhood in that sort of thing, is there? Perhaps I shouldn't have been so upset by it, but—well, I was.

"Then I went back to college, and that fall I discovered that some of my professors and a great number of my fellow students had very little interest in religion. It wasn't just a lack of interest in the particular religion that I had known as Christianity. It was a lack of interest in any religion. Some of the students said openly what I felt that many of them believed, that religion was just a form of old-fashioned foolishness, and not a part of the life of a scientific age.

"I remember an argument that I had about then with an American student. I had asked him some question about Christianity in his country, and he seemed amazed that I should have any interest in the subject.

" 'Why worry about that?' he asked me.

" 'But, didn't Christianity contribute greatly to the making of your America?' I inquired.

" 'Christianity fiddlesticks!' he exclaimed. 'Our country was made by the pioneer spirit of our forefathers, who were always pushing ahead, seeking new territory and new power. And you can be sure that Christianity had very little to do with that, whatever they may have thought about it, for a religion is always a conservative and never a pioneering thing.' "

"Yes, I have heard that same sort of talk," remarked Dr. Lo. "But you must remember that students are always doing a lot of talking that has little real understanding behind it."

"I know that, of course. And it wasn't just talking that influenced me. I kept on going to church. Once in a while somebody would ask me if I was a Christian, and I always said that I was. One summer I was a delegate to a student Christian conference.

"But all the time I kept looking at the people in the towns where I found myself. I watched the things that they did, and I tried to analyze their motives. I read the newspapers. You know the sort of things they have in them—lynchings, race riots, lawbreaking of all sorts.

"And do you know what I kept remembering? I kept remembering something that one of the missionary teachers had said to me here in China in the old school days, something that did a lot to induce me to become a Christian. I had demanded of him what superiority there was in the teaching of Jesus over that of Confucius that should make me, a Chinese, desert Confucianism for Christianity.

" 'The teachings of Confucius are very lofty,' my teacher had acknowledged. 'But how many men do you know who live up to those teachings?'

"And when I had to admit that there were not many who did so, my teacher said that right there was the difference between Confucianism and Christianity—that Confucianism had only a high standard of ethics, while Christianity offered also a power to make it possible to achieve that high standard.

"Well, what proof is there, when you study a country like America as a whole, that her Christianity gives her people any more power with which to achieve the ideals of Jesus than we have with which to achieve the ideals of Confucius? Look at the conditions in business, in politics, in society, sometimes in their very churches. Do you call them Christian?"

"Not yet," replied Dr. Lo, at which his companion shot him a quick and questioning look. Then, without demanding further enlightenment, he plunged ahead.

"I came back to China greatly upset religiously. It's hard to talk about such things, but, in my early student days, my religion had meant a lot to me. It had meant so much that I couldn't throw it overboard without a struggle. You know the condition China was in two years ago when I came home. And I used to come to these Sunday-afternoon meetings—I was even a member of one of the committees in charge—and hear men say, in all sorts of ways,

A CHRISTIAN NURSE IN DR. IDA KAHN'S HOSPITAL, NANCHANG—A
TYPE OF THE CHINESE NEW WOMAN, WHO IS SEEKING
AN OUTLET FOR TRUE SERVICE.

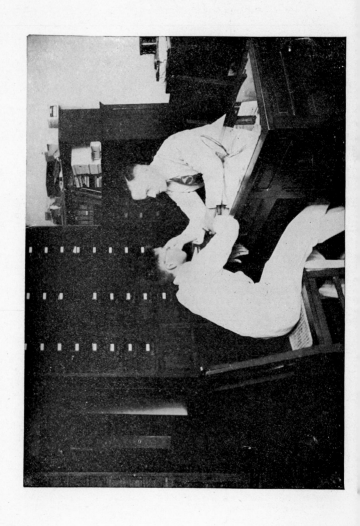

what amounted to, 'Jesus is the hope of China.'

"What made me do it is more than I know, but I began to question those statements. For what does Jesus offer China? Brotherhood, righteousness, and other fine ideals like that, all growing out of a life of universal love. And what China needs, what China must have if she is to be saved from her enemies, is not love, so helpless in a world like this, but an iron might."

"Are you sure that is what China needs?"

"How else is she to defend herself and become strong?"

"I think that there's another way. Any Christian ought to believe that there's another way. But we will not argue that. Is this iron heart *all* that China needs?"

"Of course not. There are many things."

"What are they?" Dr. Lo persisted.

"There's the spirit of scientific inquiry," Mr. Tang replied. "China needs to learn how to discover the facts about the world and life. She cannot possibly succeed in attaining strength in this scientific age without that."

"And you think that Christianity is opposed to the spirit of scientific inquiry?"

"Surely it is. Look at the unscientific beliefs they tell us we must swallow if we are to be Christians!"

"Anything else?"

"Many other things. But those are the principal ones."

[135]

"So, if I understand you correctly, you have almost lost your interest in Christianity because of the impractical nature of Christian teaching, and because you don't think that a man can be a Christian and at the same time a modern scientific thinker. Is that right?"

"That's about right."

"You must excuse me if I sound impolite, but you ought to know that such a charge is nonsense. There is no better science being taught in China just now than in some Christian colleges. Yet suppose everything you say were true. Do you know a better religion than Christianity?"

A pause.

"Do you mean, as a teaching, or as people practice it?"

"Either way. But primarily as a teaching."

"No, I know no better one."

"Then why forsake it so easily?"

"I'm not." The words shot back with a deadly earnestness that could not be mistaken. "That's why I came back to the service today. I am not ready to cut loose yet. But, Doctor, it isn't so much a case with me of Christianity as compared with other religions. The question that torments me is this, Why any religion at all?"

And the two passed on, deep in a discussion such as occupies many minds in China today. For in the changes that are coming in China, there is nowhere a deeper stirring than in the realm of religion. Here it is that, finally, the most profound impression may be made upon Chinese character. And to many Chinese this struggle, as it resolves itself, is becoming not one between a new religion and older faiths, but between religion and no faith. It is a struggle for faith itself upon which China is entering.

China has never been a nation overly given to religious contemplation. There have, to be sure, been thousands of Chinese who have withdrawn from life to build up the health of their souls in some quiet monastery. But the Chinese have never lived in the religious atmosphere that has been characteristic, for example, of India. As a whole, they have been rather material-minded, thinking more about the securing of rice and the success of business than the favor of the gods. Indeed, the favor of the gods has been largely sought that the other material gains might be assured.

To a large degree, the influence of Confucius and his disciples has been responsible for this hard-headed attitude toward life. The first interest of the great sages was in laying out patterns of conduct that would bring men peace, well-being, and the respect of their fellows in this life. Confucius himself refused to talk about any other life when pressed by his followers, pleading that he knew too little about this. Reduced to its essence, the teaching of the Great Master came to this—that if a man would watch with care his conduct in this existence, the future would care for itself.

Yet along with this rather circumscribed outlook —what might be termed a true agnosticism—there has gone a popular belief in the reality of a spiritual world that has made the Chinese unwilling to be content with a mere philosophy, and has caused them, in their temples, to experiment with all kinds of religious approaches. Thus it has come to pass that while the Chinese has been, at bottom, a good deal of a materialist, he has also given devoted allegiance to several systems of faith.

Writers about the religions of China generally mention three—Confucianism, Taoism, Buddhism.

Confucianism, as the Chinese students are today insisting, is really not a religion at all. Confucius would have been of all men most horrified had he been told that, after his death, the attempt would be made to deify him, and to set up a method of soul salvation based upon his precepts. But that happened. Confucius left, not a religion, but a philosophy. His great gift to China was a set of ethical principles which, if followed, would insure peace in the State and good-will among men. To this day, there are no idols in Confucian temples; only the simple tablets bearing the names and honors of the Great Master and his leading disciples.

The fate that befell Confucianism is an illuminating commentary on the insatiable demand of the human soul for an object of worship. The great teacher died almost five hundred years before the birth of Christ, a disappointed man whose wisdom had been rejected by almost all the rulers of China. His immediate followers determined to perpetuate his teachings, and, as the years passed, they began to shine forth for the lofty precepts that they were. Within a few hundred years what had begun as veneration for a sage began to take on the elements of worship. And since then, at sporadic intervals, there have been attempts to present this teaching as a code of religion, with the modest teacher of old exalted to a place in the heavens.

Lao-tze, the founder of Taoism, was a contemporary of Confucius, but a different sort of man. He was a mystic, and as eager to dwell in the world of spirits as Confucius was glad to keep out of it. Lao-tze tried to explain the inner mystery at the core of life with a mystical term, much as did the author of the Fourth Gospel in the New Testament. That writer used a Greek term, the Logos, that we have never been able to translate satisfactorily into English. Lao-tze used a Chinese term, the Tao, that also defies complete translation. Perhaps the term "way" is as good a rendering as any. So Lao-tze left China Taoism, or the religion of the way of salvation.

But, in the course of thousands of years, the religion of Taoism has suffered a sad decline. Lao-tze was a pure-hearted mystic, in whose teachings are to be found many beautiful and true things. But when men come to deal too familiarly with the mystical, it is easy to decline from the spiritual to the spiritualistic. And so Taoism has come to be nothing more than a secret necromancy, by which the spirits that people the universe can be placated and good luck secured for him who patronizes the priests.

Buddhism is the great missionary religion of the East. Born of the spiritual search of Gautama in India, it came over the mountains to China not long after other apostles had begun to take another religion westward. Today there is little Buddhism left in India proper, but in all eastern Asia it profoundly affects millions of lives.

There is something in the fundamental assumptions of Buddhism that will always appeal to the mind of the East. For the great revelation that was given to Gautama was that men are without peace in heart because they are chained to the "wheel of desire," which bears them endlessly through a round of torments, and that peace is simply the abandonment of all desire and the giving of oneself to untroubled contemplation. The gift that Buddhism offers the perplexed is, therefore, the art of "letting go," of seeing the emptiness of the concerns of life, and of becoming self-composed. When the devotee has achieved perfectly this power of self-containment, he becomes a Buddha, "an enlightened one." Until that time, he remains on the wheel of life, passing through one incarnation after another.

[140]

Two other religions must also be mentioned when talking of the faith of the Chinese.

Mohammedanism came to China while Mohammed still lived. It has known periods of great favor, but for centuries now the Mohammedans have lived distinct from the rest of the Chinese. There are about five times as many Mohammedans in China as Christians, but there is no missionary fervor among them. They are to be found in large numbers in such an outlying province as Kansu, and in smaller colonies in the cities, where they carry on trades that are restricted to Mohammedans, and live in quarters as distinct as a Jewish ghetto in the West.

The real religion of millions of Chinese is none of these, but animism. This animism may have been influenced to some degree by one of the other faiths. In truth, modern Taoism is practically animism. For the mass of the humble folk of China, religion consists in knowing the names of the spirits that fill the atmosphere, in discovering what it is that makes most of them so malignant, and in carrying on such sacrifices or ceremonies as shall keep these spirits in good humor.

It is impossible for the Westerner to understand the common Chinese fear of malignant spirits until he has lived in the midst of it. Indeed, he may live in it for years and never realize the hold which it has upon his native neighbors. For it would be impossible, in the limits of such a book as this, even to catalog the devils and evil spirits that people the very air for the average Chinese. But there they are, millions of them. They hover around every motion of every waking hour, and they enter the sanctity of sleep. An intricate system of circumventing them, that makes the streets twist in a fashion to daze Boston's legendary cow and puts walls in front of doors to belie the hospitality within, runs throughout the social order. The pursuit of this system is the real religion of millions.

There are large parts of China where Taoism, as an organized form of worship, is disappearing. There are no regular services in the temples, and the priests are seen usually in the funeral processions of wealthy people who patronize all the creeds in order to assure the deceased the benefit which any may be able to give. But the belief in spirits upon which Taoism battens will not be gone for a long, long time. And the Christian who reads in the newspapers that the Senate of the United States has adjourned so that it may not be forced to do business on Friday the thirteenth, will hardly expect to see the power of Chinese superstition pass in this generation.

The rapidly decreasing reputation of the Buddhist priesthood points to the eventual disappearance of the Buddhist religion. No faith can finally survive whose servants do not exhibit elements of moral strength greater than those possessed by the run of men. There have been attempts at a Buddhist revival in many parts of China recently. Within some of the monasteries the sympathetic searcher may still find sweet and simple spirits, the purity of whose lives and the ardor of whose religious passion command respect. And so long as Buddhism can produce such lives *at all*, it is entitled to respectful consideration.

But these are not the aspects of Buddhism that the masses of Chinese see. They see the ignorant, lazy, often immoral parasites who make up the mass of the two million Buddhist priests. The *Ho-shan* (priest) with his endless pursuit of easy money and an easy life is as much the butt of the tea-room satirist as was the overfed friar of the medieval storyteller of Europe.

There are some truths in Buddhism that will live in the faith of China for all time, but the unworthy priesthood is the best indication that these truths must find their final home, their fulfilment, in a purer spiritual atmosphere. In many centers men are seldom to be seen in the Buddhist temples today, and when there, they are apt to be in an apologetic mood. Yet, in the deepest moments of life, when death enters the household, it is seldom that the priests are not summoned.

The somnolence that seems to have befallen Confucianism should not deceive anyone as to its power. The philosophy that has molded a civilization for twenty-five hundred years is not going to pass away in a decade. It is true that recent attempts to revive

Confucianism as a national worship have not been successful. But that does not change the fact that Confucianism, with its doctrine of the golden mean, by which men are guarded against excess of any kind, and its morality designed to bring reward in this life, underlies the thinking of every Chinese who thinks at all. And, as the philosophy of the Chinese, Confucianism will live on. It is a wonderful philosophy, and much better adapted to the practical working out of a Kingdom of Heaven on earth than most of the philosophy that has come from Western lands.

There need be no bitter conflict between Christianity and Confucianism. With spiritual needs satisfied elsewhere, Confucianism will become what its founder intended it to be, the system of thought by which the Chinese orders the affairs of his daily life. Teachings which do not conform to the demands of the present—and no system can stand without change for twenty-five centuries—will be modified by the words of later disciples. A century hence the Chinese leader will be as quick to acknowledge the abiding value of many of the lessons taught by the greatest sage of his race as he will be to proclaim his place among the disciples of that other Master.

For it is impossible to talk of the religious revolution that is taking place in China without telling of the growth of the power of this other Master. In the previous chapters of this book we have caught glimpses of the influence, both direct and indirect, that Christianity has exerted in transforming Chinese life to its depths. It is a thrilling story—this of the growth of the religion of the Cross in this mighty land.

Christianity first came to China not long after Buddhism, borne by certain emissaries of the Nestorian branch of the Eastern Church. What it accomplished then we cannot tell, for the only record that we have is a short inscription graven on a single stone tablet.

Later, at the time that Protestantism was coming to life in Western Europe, those hardy Catholic pioneers, the Jesuits, penetrated China. Their great leader, St. Francis Xavier, died before the gates had opened. In all missionary history, perhaps, there is no more poignant cry than that of Xavier as, after his days of achievement in India, Ceylon, Japan, he lay dying on a little island off that China coast that had repelled him, and cried in desperation, "O rock, rock! wilt thou never break?"

The rock has broken. The Jesuit missions became entangled in questions that bordered on politics (curiously enough, these grew out of a dispute over the proper Chinese character with which to express the Christian name for God) and were sternly repressed for centuries. In 1807, however, the first Protestant missionary, Robert Morrison, reached Canton, and after that the way opened more and more for Christian effort.

The growth of the Christian Church in China has been phenomenal. When Robert Morrison lay dying, after twenty-seven years of as devoted labor as any man ever gave to the cause of the Kingdom, he gathered the other missionaries about him, and, as they reviewed the less than twenty converts that they had secured in more than a quarter of a century, they agreed that it was scarcely to be hoped that there could be a thousand baptized Christians at the close of a century. Yet when the century of effort ended, despite the bloody massacre of Christians that fell upon the young Church just seven years before that anniversary, it was discovered that there were 179,000 Protestant church members in good standing! And when an enumeration was made again in 1922, only fifteen years after the Morrison Centenary, it was found that the church membership had grown in the interval to about four hundred thousand, with twenty-five thousand Chinese pastors caring for them.

It is said that the Church is growing at a more rapid rate in China today than in any other part of the Protestant world. Practically every mission reports that there are more seekers after truth than can be cared for by the present forces. For years Christian missionaries called upon their supporters in America and other lands to pray that the doors of China might be opened. No doubt you have heard some of those prayers. Today they have been answered, and the embarrassment that besets the workers is as to how, with circumscribed forces, they are to take advantage of the unprecedented opportunities thus presented.

Christianity is certainly the most aggressive religious force in China today. Its influence is being felt in all these realms of Chinese life of which we have already spoken—in education, in social customs, in the life of Chinese women, and in industry. There are Christian evangelistic centers of some kind in four fifths of all the counties (1,704) of China. And the power of Christianity is clearly on the side of the forces that are making for an intelligent, self-reliant, prosperous nation.

But the great opposition that the Christian worker has to face in China just now is not that of the old faiths. It is the opposition of those who say that all religion tends to superstition, and that a modern and enlightened nation will build its life without giving religion a place.

This does not necessarily mean a plea for the adoption of materialism. There have been Chinese who have argued that a thoroughgoing materialism, seeking material benefits at whatever cost and through the power of a militaristically organized state, offered the only hope of strength in a world like ours. But the Chinese have a fundamental distrust, growing out of their long generations of disregard for the soldier, of a program like that. Besides, there have been enough examples in the world of late to prove that a militaristic materialism, while it may succeed for a time, does not guarantee the enduring good fortune of a people.

Yet, rejecting materialism, there are many Chinese who would likewise reject religion. The chancellor of the National University of Peking, Tsai Yuan-pei, one of the most influential men in China today, is one of these. A hero to most of China's students, and a man of unblemished character, Chancellor Tsai has dismissed religion—any religion, all religion—as simply a survival from some lower stage of man's development, and has suggested that, for the educated modern, the place once filled by religion should be taken by some form of esthetics and ethics. Perhaps ethical culture is the term that comes closest to expressing what Chancellor Tsai has in mind.

The strength of this movement toward "no religion" is underestimated by many of the people who have not penetrated under the surface of Chinese student life. But when you talk with a group of thinking Chinese, you will not go far without discovering that they are questioning the very foundations of religion. This is true even in student bodies that have been under direct religious influence.

Two or three years ago a Chinese friend and I tried to find out what students were asking in the higher grade mission schools in eastern China. Questions such as these proved the common ones:

"Why should we have religion since it is superstition that causes stagnation in progress?"

"Is not socialism better for China than Christianity?"

"Is not belief in immortality a kind of superstition?"

"How can we believe in the miracles (of the Bible)? To the scientific point of view, they are absolutely untrue."

A bishop friend of mine went out to the province of Szechwan not long ago, on the western border of China. If anywhere, you would have expected such ideas to have made little progress in that remote section. Yet when he asked what the Szechwanese students were thinking about, he received such queries as these:

"Is the existence of the human soul true?"

"Is there a real and imperishable soul left after the death of any person?"

"Can the soul consciously sense itself?"

"What is the real aim of the missionaries who travel about China?"

Early in 1922 there came to Peking student delegates from more than twenty nations, to hold a convention of the World's Student Christian Federation. Certainly there was more than ordinary significance in the holding of such a gathering in the old Chinese capital. Perhaps the Chinese who would face the new day without religious allegiances sensed this, for they greeted the delegates from abroad in an extremely aggressive manner. Significantly enough, this movement took the form of organizing anti-Christian federations, thus demonstrating the way in which, in the minds of the students, the cause of religion has come to be identified, for the future, with that of Christianity. Most of the activities of the anti-Christian forces at that time consisted of issuing proclamations, denouncing religion as superstition. But since then the movement away from religion has taken a more serious turn.

At the annual conference of the Association for the Advancement of Education, for instance, the commission on problems of elementary education brought in a resolution urging all teachers not to teach religion in any way in any elementary school, and especially not to teach such a belief as that there is a Supreme Being in the universe, as a thing which has not been proved and cannot be proved. The resolution, adopted by the Association, has been sent broadcast over China. The standing of the Association among teachers is very high.

But while the forces that would wean China away from all religion are thus showing strength, the forces that make for faith are likewise gaining. Especially is this true of the Christian Church. We have already mentioned its rapid numerical growth. There are other, and more striking, signs of increasing power.

Most hopeful of all is the increase in responsibility upon the part of the Chinese themselves. For a century the Protestant work in China was the work of "missions." Devoted men and women crossed the seas to spend their lives in service for the Chinese. About them there gathered groups of converts, but the control of the enterprise was always in the hands of the missionary. Today this is rapidly changing. The groups of converts are becoming self-conscious churches. The "native helpers" are becoming self-reliant pastors. The missionary is becoming an adviser who works with and through others, rather than a man who must bear all the great burdens alone. In other words, the years of planting are bringing forth their harvest of an indigenous Chinese Christianity.

This transformation, which amounts almost to a revolution within Chinese Christianity, was graphically illustrated at the National Christian Conference which met in 1922. Fifteen years earlier, when the centenary of Morrison's landing was celebrated with a similar gathering, it was called a National *Missionary* Conference, and every single delegate was a foreigner. Now it has become a National *Christian* Conference, and more than half of the thousand delegates (omitting the visitors from abroad) are Chinese! There is a Chinese chairman. Chinese act as chairmen of the important commissions and committees. The basic report, that seeks to express "The Message of the Church to China," is written entirely by Chinese. And when it seems that differing conceptions of the mission of the Church may bring a rift into the gathering, it is a Chinese, dean of a theological seminary in Peking,

Dr. Timothy T. Lew, who paints the picture of the Church upon which all can unite. That picture is so remarkable that we give it here, not only as a picture of what the Christian Church in China hopes to be, but as a picture of what the Christian Church should be around the world:

"First of all, the Chinese Christian Church shall be a fearless fighter against sin.

"Second, the Chinese Christian Church shall be a faithful interpreter of Jesus.

"Third, the Chinese Christian Church shall stand as a flaming prophet of God.

"Fourth, the Chinese Christian Church shall be a worthy teacher of the Bible. She shall not in the least fear, but, on the contrary, even welcome scientific investigation, and the most critical study any human being has the wisdom or folly to put to its pages. She shall not show any anxiety for the Bible by any negative means or unnecessary attempts to put a human fence around the eternal truth of God for its protection. Not the Bible alone, but all the teachings of the Church, she shall gladly submit to any true scientific tests and trials. She shall stand by the seeker of truth and bend over the reverent inquiring hearts as a divine pedagogue sent from God, with dauntless courage and divine patience to teach and guide as the Master used to do when he said to his disciples, 'Come and see.'

"Fifth, the Chinese Church shall be a genuine servant to the Chinese people.

"Sixth, the Chinese Church shall be a defender of Christian unity and comprehensiveness. She shall stand for, nay, even fight for, unity in diversity, jealously to guard against any encroachment on the comprehensiveness which is her glory, her witness, and her power.

"Under her protecting wings everyone shall find a place, Peter and John, Paul and Barnabas, and even the critical and doubting Thomas, for Christ is with her, his love constrains her members, his presence insures her safety. She shall teach her members to agree to differ but resolve to love."

To a large extent, the battle between religion and no religion that is being fought in China today is the same battle that is being fought in other parts of the world. And the outcome everywhere will be the same. "Mankind is incurably religious." The need for strength beyond our own is felt in every land. The demand for faith will triumph over all other demands.

In China this means that, in days to come, as the Chinese Church becomes increasingly self-reliant, its faith will become increasingly that of multitudes of Chinese. Already, when there are but four hundred thousand Protestant Christians among four hundred million people, it is astonishing how large a place the little group has come to fill in the life of the nation. When, for example, a Shanghai weekly last year held an open voting contest as to the twelve outstanding living Chinese, four on the list selected were acknowledged Christians, and five others were men who had shown much interest in Christianity.

The Christianity of China's future will be Chinese Christianity. It will be expressed by Chinese minds. It will emphasize the teachings that are most needed to meet China's spiritual needs. It will show traces of the influences of all the great teachings of China's past, just as our own faith shows the influence of the teachings that molded the men who bequeathed us our civilization. But in loyalty to Christ and in determination to exalt Him as Lord, Chinese Christianity will be as genuine an expression of faith as the Christianity of any other part of the world.

VIII

AMERICA AND CHINA'S REVOLUTION

In the days that followed the Manchu downfall a dozen years ago, Yuan Shih-kai, China's first permanent president, gave an audience to Dr. H. H. Lowry, at that time president of Peking University.

"You missionaries are responsible for this revolution," the Chinese leader said. "Now you must see us through."

Dr. Lowry protested. "Your excellency, I have been in China almost forty years. In all that time I can assure you that it has been a cardinal principle of missionary policy never to interfere in Chinese politics. Whatever our sympathies may have been, you may be sure that the missionaries took no part in the recent political upheaval."

"That may be so," the President replied. "But you are responsible, none the less. For what have you been doing during these forty years, you and your associates? You have been teaching that there is one true God, before whom all men stand as equal brothers. And you cannot teach that kind of doctrine without leading to the sort of revolution that we have had in China."

There was an undeniable basis of truth in the charge made by the Chinese President. Any serious acceptance of the Christian doctrine of the father-

[155]

hood of God and brotherhood of man does have immediate relation to earthly despotisms. The gospel truly is, as Lowell said, dynamite, likely at any time to blow to pieces any ancient order.

The Manchu throne was near to falling about the time of the American Civil War, when a Chinese enthusiast was fired with a strangely disordered perception of Christian ideas and launched the bloody Taiping rebellion. For almost two decades the rebels held much of the heart of the country, to be defeated at last only after more lives had been lost than fell in the battles of the World War.

The end of the Manchus finally came a half century later, when a revolt, that started without planning among troops stationed in Wuchang, spread until, without much fighting, the boy-emperor left his throne. The men and women who bore a leading part in that revolution were, in instance after instance, persons who in schools and churches had been under Christian influence. The missionary must accept a measure of responsibility for the changes in the Far East since the opening of this century.

America, likewise, must acknowledge some responsibility for, as well as interest in, China's revolution. Since the opening to the West, it has been America that has been most near to capturing the Chinese imagination. Thousands of Chinese have studied in America. Other thousands have worked there. Near the city of Canton, for instance, there is a whole district largely inhabited by Chinese who have lived in America. It is more than a coincidence that Canton and its environs are a center of Chinese political progressivism.

China, in her basic political life, which is the organization of her villages, has always been democratic. It remained, however, for America to demonstrate that the whole national life could be formed on a democratic model. And it was largely the American example that moved China to launch out upon her present governmental experiment.

Moreover, America has an enormous interest in the success of this Chinese experiment because of the relative position of the two countries. The recognition of the importance of the Pacific Basin in world politics has become a commonplace. More than two years ago the Powers testified to this by their willingness to submit their military and naval programs to the review of a Washington Conference. A glance at this strategic Pacific Basin shows that the two largest nations that touch it are America and China. China is still mighty, from the standpoint of modern states, only in its potentialities. But the safety of democracy in the world is bound to be enormously influenced, one way or the other, by the measure of success that attends the democratic experiment in China.

If the western rim of the Pacific Basin shall see a strong, pacific democracy in control, spreading its message of government of, by, and for the people back to the very heart of Asia, the cause of democracy in all the world will be strengthened. But if there shall be only the mockery of a people's hopes, and a mounting disorder that leads at last to the substitution of a new despotism for the old, the hope for a democratic world-order will suffer accordingly. Therefore it behooves America in her foreign policy to put at the forefront the wise support of every effort that makes for the building of a permanent democracy in the republic that faces her across the Pacific.

Of course, when President Yuan Shih-kai spoke to Dr. Lowry, he had in mind only the political revolution that had substituted a president for an emperor. And when we speak of the wisdom of giving support to the democratic movement in China, some will consider that only a call to political action. But those who have read this book will know that China's revolution concerns many a realm other than the political, and that the challenge to our support comes from fields seldom mentioned in the newspaper despatches.

We have seen that China's revolution has been passing through a military phase, but that now there is beginning to be a reassertion of the ancient supremacy of the educated man, who would found a new state on deeper, more transforming changes. So we have seen a revolution that, by making learning democratic, is changing the cultural outlook for the entire nation. We have seen a revolution that dares to test old customs, beliefs, and social standards, to see if they are fit to survive in a democratic and scientific age. We have seen a revolution that proclaims a new day for womanhood. We have seen a revolution that includes the growth of a new order of industry, with all its attendant problems. We have seen a revolution that even leads to a religious crisis, with men hesitating between committing their spiritual welfare to a new faith or rejecting all belief in religion. And out of every one of these changes there comes the call for sympathy, understanding, and support.

Primarily, of course, these problems of change are to be solved by the Chinese if they are ever solved at all. The outsider may point to experiences in the history of his own nation that hold suggestive value, or he may go further by giving encouragement to the men and women who are following what seem to him the best lines of advance. But the basic work and the mass of work must be done by the people directly involved.

No foreigner, however well intentioned, can place Chinese leadership in the hands of the educated men and women who are fit for that leadership. It must be these men and women who themselves demonstrate their ability and take that leadership. No foreigner can reform the social abuses of China. It must be Chinese who, speaking as patriots, make the abuses clear and lead in their abolition. No foreigner can protect China from the ills of a conscience-less industrialism. It must be Chinese who bring to pass an industrial order that escapes the pitfalls other nations have not escaped. No foreigner can give the final answer to China's spiritual problems. It must be Chinese who, pioneering like all the great hearts of the ages, lead their people into light. In all these and other realms the foreigner may have valuable advice to give. But the burden of the change must finally be borne by Chinese.

Yet this does not absolve the rest of the world from doing what is possible for the help of the Chinese. Out of self-interest, if for no higher motive, men in other lands should be filled with concern to see that China has the maximum of their help in this hour of change. For if there is any one fact as to the relation of nations that is being forced home upon us in these days, it is the fact of interdependence. The mechanical advances that have so lessened the difficulties of intercommunication have made it more true than ever that no nation lives unto itself, and that all are concerned in the good or ill of any. If this is true anywhere, how certainly it must be true in the case of a nation that comprises a quarter of the world's population!

A few years ago there broke out in northern China an epidemic of the most dreadful disease known to medical science, the pneumonic plague. As far as the records show, there has never been a case in which a person has contracted this form of plague and recovered. And it is very easily contracted. But medical missionaries and well-trained Chinese physicians threw themselves into the work of isolation so promptly that, although thousands died, the area of devastation was held to a small part of North China.

A few years later there broke out on the steppes of interior Asia a much milder form of disease, capable of cure by timely medical attention. There were no modern-trained doctors in that region, however, so that the epidemic gained such headway that it swept around the world and, known as the Spanish influenza, destroyed more lives than the World War.

The world's experience with the pneumonic plague and with the Spanish influenza is a parable. The time has passed when there can be political, social, or moral sickness in any part of the globe, and all the world not be in danger. The sufferings of Russian mouzhiks under the knout may not have seemed, yesterday, a matter of importance to men in other nations. Today we know better. And the happiness or wretchedness of the great mass called Chinese may not seem, at this hour, to have any close connection with the welfare of other peoples. But tomorrow the interrelationship will be clear.

The forces that are working for the making of a better China face tremendous odds. As those students go out to build a new nation on the firm foundation of popular education, they face the inertia of centuries, with the active opposition of most of the men controlling governmental revenues. As new opportunities are sought for China's women, the entrenched conservatism of forty centuries rises up in combative alarm. As men are told of new sources of inner strength, there is always to be felt the holding back of the feeling that "what was good enough for Grandfather is good enough for me."

Just because these difficulties do stand in the way, we should be the more eager to bear such help as is possible to the servants of new China. And there are definite things that we can do that will directly benefit. This help can be given in two directions, in China and at home.

Obviously, one immediate way of supporting the effort to change China's life in its fundamentals is to give to the Christian enterprise in China such backing as it has never had in the past. We can all rejoice at the rapid growth of the Christian community. The question sometimes asked as to the worth of Christian missions has been answered by the Chinese who throng the mission stations in a more emphatic manner than any others could answer it. But the time has not yet come when the Christian forces have been able to respond to more than a small part of the calls that have come to them.

Two years ago, in connection with the meeting of the National Christian Conference, there was completed the most thorough survey ever made of any foreign-mission field. The results of that survey have been published in a great volume called *The Christian Occupation of China*. The book is much larger than most world atlases. But if you were to study the mass of facts in that volume carefully, you would discover that, despite the remarkable achievements of Christianity in China up to this time, there remain vast regions to be evangelized. Areas aggregating eight hundred and nineteen thousand square miles of China, for instance, still lie more than ten miles from any Christian center. More than 430,000 square miles for which missions have acknowledged responsibility for years is still relatively unoccupied. And in places that are called "occupied," there are so few workers that only the most elemental form of effort is possible.

There is a portion of the province of Szechwan, for example, for which the Methodist Episcopal Church has assumed responsibility. This is one of the strong missions, and the territory in question is strategic, lying in the heart of the province, athwart its main artery of travel, and containing about 12,500,000 people. The foreign missionary force is ten, but all but two of these are held continually to the direction of institutions that make it impossible for them to do any itinerant preaching. There are seventy churches and chapels and forty schools, but these do not begin to meet the need. Each chapel has a preaching service once every few weeks, but the rest of the time it has nothing to offer. The press of inquirers is so great that a rule had to be adopted three years ago limiting the number of church members to be received in any year to a quarter of the total already on the rolls, because of the lack of facilities to train the new converts.

No one would call this adequate occupation of this area, yet this is one of the best-worked sections of West China. The same story might be repeated from almost every part of the country, and it would not be confined to lack of evangelistic equipment.

Take the situation in the field of medical missions, one of the proved methods of making Christian benevolence clear. The China Medical Missionary Association has wisely judged that the minimum requirements for a mission hospital with fifty beds are two foreign doctors and one foreign nurse. But if the missions were to attempt to reach this standard, China would need three hundred additional physicians and two hundred additional registered nurses immediately. One half of the mission hospitals in China are still without the services of any foreign registered nurse, while thirty-four per cent have no trained nurses of any kind, Chinese or foreign. Eighty per cent of the mission hospitals had only one foreign or foreign-trained Chinese doctor when this survey was made.

When the survey was made, there were ninety Chinese cities previously unoccupied within which missions had officially voted to open mission stations within five years. There were thirty-nine cities within which new hospitals were to be erected. These plans had been approved by the boards supporting these missions. But their carrying out would require a large increase in the support of the missionary cause.

"One fourth of the total area of China's eighteen provinces remains uncared for by any Protestant missionary or Chinese home missionary agency," says Milton T. Stauffer, the man who edited the survey. "In addition, an area exceeding in extent the whole of China's eighteen provinces and embracing almost all of Inner Mongolia, Outer Mongolia, Sinkiang, Kokonor, Chwanpien and Tibet, still remains neglected and practically unentered. To these great stretches of unworked territory we must add the cities of Indo-China, Formosa, the East Indies, and other places where the Chinese, estimated at over eight million, reside and where as yet comparatively little evangelistic work is done. Eighty-six per cent of Kansu, seventy-seven per cent of Manchuria, and seventy-five per cent of Kwangsi—if greater definiteness be needed to press home the point—are still outside the acknowledged responsibility of any Christian evangelizing agency. Two thirds of all the counties of China (1,704) average less than five communicants per ten thousand inhabitants. One fifth report not a single evangelistic center. The missionaries giving full-time service to the evangelization of China's ten million Moslems can be counted on the fingers of one hand. There are approximately twelve million tribespeople in Western and Southwestern China. These simple people are eager for the gospel message. Missionaries are welcome where Chinese Christian workers might find it difficult to work among them. Wherever the gospel has been preached, mass movements have resulted. Only the missionaries are too few—hardly one among 200,000."

The immense field still awaiting Christian effort in China was suggested by some of the appeals that accompanied the information sent to the men formulating the survey. From a European missionary in a lonely station in Mongolia came these words: "The Christian churches and mission societies have left the whole of Mongolia to us. We cannot get even one missionary to relieve us (for furlough). If you can do anything for Mongolia, please do it, and do it at once."

From Kansu, where the Moslem problem is most difficult, a young English worker wrote: "Every missionary is conscious of unoccupied areas. They extend from our very front doors, nay, from our private rooms, through innumerable districts and towns out into the desert silences of Sinkiang and Tibet. It is no sudden, spasmodic, individual business that will solve the problem; only a prayerful united effort, in which we all share heartily and to the full."

What is to be our share in this prayerful and united effort? Is it to be the devotion of more of our income for the support of the enterprise? Yes, for many of us this will undoubtedly be a part that we can play. If we take our maps and draw a pencil hurriedly across the spots that we have mentioned as still inadequately occupied or unoccupied, and then remember that there are other regions that have not been here named, we will see that the mere business of bringing Christian opportunity to all China will require vastly more support than we have so far given the missionary cause.

But to some of us the responsibility will not cease with the giving of more money. Money alone will not provide that new spiritual outlook which makes the complete transformation of the country possible. There must be a devotion of life that will reach into our colleges and professional schools and make the strongest students there face the demand: "Where can you better serve your generation than in such a center of world change as this republic across the Pacific?"

The feeling sometimes expressed, that the end of the missionary enterprise is at hand, can hardly survive in the light of the unoccupied fields we have mentioned. Just to keep the missionary force at its present level requires constant reinforcement, and the entering of new territory will increase the call. These missionaries, who must work hand in hand with Chinese Christians of fine training and devoted spirit, must be of as high caliber as it is possible for us to produce. As the Chinese dean of the theological seminary of Peking University said recently, "Do not stop sending missionaries, but send us better ones."

There is no more outstanding Christian in China today than Dr. Cheng Ching-yi, who was the chairman of the National Christian Conference of 1922. Last year Dr. Cheng had an opportunity to discuss this matter of missionary recruits with the leaders of the mission boards of America and Canada, and this is what he said:

"The Church is seeking more missionaries. It is far from our purpose to give the impression that the coming forward of Chinese means that the missionaries are to retire from the scene and that more of them are not needed. . . . There is a real need of, and room for, more new missionaries in China. In a sense, they are needed today more than ever before.

"But a word is necessary regarding the missionaries who are needed in China under the new conditions that have arisen. In addition to possessing spiritual and intellectual qualifications, the missionary of today needs thoroughly to understand that his task is to assist the Chinese Church, and to be willing to help, not to boss, his Chinese fellow workers. We need, therefore, those who possess a broad and sympathetic heart, and are able to form real friendship with the Chinese.

"We need those who can see and appreciate all that is good, and beautiful, and true, wherever it is found. We need those who are willing to learn, as well as to teach, and who are prepared to work with the Chinese or even under them. We need those who have a real understanding of, and desire for, international brotherhood, and the spirit of tolerance with those who differ from them. In a word, we need missionaries who are after the heart of God to 'Come over and help us.' . . .

"The present situation is certainly different from that of former days, but the need is just as great and urgent, if not more so. We want friends; we desire partners and comrades; we seek for cooperation and sympathy. The work has never been so interesting and full of promise as it is today. All its problems and difficulties are but so many attractions, that draw the men and women of vision and of a daring spirit to answer this magnificent and worthy call from afar."

A third way by which we may help in the making of the new China is by making clear our readiness to pass over control of the Christian work in China as rapidly as possible to the Chinese. Dr. Cheng hinted at that when he spoke of the need for missionaries who would be "willing to help, not to boss." The question is a ticklish one, and will, in its details, involve matters of missionary administration that we need not trouble about here. It is the main principle that now confronts us.

We must remember that Protestantism is now more than a hundred years old in China. This means that there are hundreds of third-generation Christians in the country—young men and women who have never lived in an atmosphere of idolatry, but have been reared from the day of birth amid Christian surroundings. Many of these have received a college and professional school education. They have an understanding of the way in which Chinese approach problems that the missionary, even after years of experience, seldom attains. And they are as eager to make China Christian as we could ever be. Some of them are members of families that have suffered heavily for Christ's sake.

We should rejoice that such a group has come to the front, and that it is constantly growing. We should recognize as the crowning evidence of the success of the missionary labors of past years the requests of these Chinese Christians for an increasing measure of responsibility in church leadership. And when they ask for the privilege of laying out the plans by which the Church is to advance, we should see that here we have the beginning of that indigenous Church that is always the goal of missionary effort. A child learns to walk by being given a chance to toddle alone. The child may stumble and trip and fall. As he staggers back and forth he may sometimes look a bit ludicrous, and we may stretch out a steadying finger. But we know better than to lift the child off the floor, for, with all his clumsiness, *that is the way in which to learn to walk*, and there is no other! Just so must it be with this child among the churches. And we can do no better to hasten a new day in China than to make it easy for this infant Church to assume control of its own life, and, even though we may occasionally stretch out a helpful finger, show the Christians of China that we have faith in their ability.

Finally, we can help the making of a new China by continually studying and agitating that China may be freed from the evils that the West has pressed upon her. The story of the dealings of Western nations with China is not comfortable reading. For almost a century now that land has felt that considerations of justice and square dealing were being outraged by nations that possessed superior military force. Nor has this sort of treatment been confined to the European nations, as Americans have sometimes tried to tell themselves. Last year Mr. Tyler Dennett wrote an exhaustive study, made from original official documents, on *Americans in Eastern Asia,*[1] and when he came to the close of its seven hundred pages he was forced to this judgment: "No nation, either of the East or West, has escaped the valid charge of bad faith. . . . Each nation, the United States not excepted, has made its contribution to the welter of evil which now comprises the Far Eastern question."

We will admit, if we will think but a moment, that, in the usual course of history, China's revolution, with its accompanying unrest, is likely to last for years yet to come. No other nation has ever attempted a change in its life without a similar period of disorder. Even the United States—although at

[1] Tyler Dennett, The Macmillan Co., New York, 1923. $5.00.

the time of its revolution there were but three million people, with a comparatively high degree of culture living in a virgin territory—went through years of struggle that really did not end until 1865. What, then, is to be expected of a revolution among a quarter of our race, most of these without education, and spread across the heart of a continent long inhabited?

Understanding and sympathy for these apostles of a new day in China will come only if we make a point of knowing what they are doing. That will require constant study, but there are books and magazines that make such study possible and easy. Some measure of the reality of our desire to become world citizens may be found in the extent to which we do this definite thing whereby the struggle for a better China may be aided.

There are at least three equally definite things that can be done in America to help forward a new day in China. Some of these have already been started, but all of them can be developed to a degree hitherto unreached.

We can, for one thing, provide the best we have in the way of advanced training for Chinese leaders. The movement that began about forty years ago, when the first group of Chinese students came to this country, and received such an impetus with the devotion of a portion of the Boxer indemnity funds to the same purpose, should be still more greatly extended. The action of the churches, in uniting for the support of several great union universities in China, and of such a body as the China Medical Board, in placing in Peking one of the world's finest medical schools, will put a first-class modern education at the disposal of hundreds of Chinese who could not cross the ocean. But there will be hundreds of others who will answer the lure of study abroad. When these come to us, whether in our schools or for that practical schooling that many now seek in an industrial plant, we must make available for them the best that we have. It is impossible to gauge the ultimate effect of such training.

Not so long ago I picked up a pamphlet. It told of the work of the Christian Association that has been formed among the Chinese college students in America. This association is not very old. In the pamphlet I found a picture of its first convention, held in Rochester, New York, in 1909. Now, that does not seem very long ago, does it? You would not expect much to have been accomplished by a group of college students since 1909, would you? But as I glanced at that photograph, I found there a man who was later China's oustanding delegate at the Paris Peace Conference, and her representative in the delicate task of taking back Shantung Province from Japanese control; a man who is the president of one of her two largest government universities; a man who is at the head of the scientific demonstration department of her National Y.M.C.A.; a man who is one of the leading professors of St. John's University, a school notable for the number of national leaders it has produced. And there were among those twenty or thirty students still others who have already contributed largely to the making of a new China. All since 1909!

A second definite contribution that we can make in America is to take steps to see that the conditions in our schools and towns do not outrage the expectations of the Chinese who come to us looking for an example of Christian civilization. The experience of the Chinese told about in a previous chapter of this book is not an unusual experience. Too many Chinese bring to America the loftiest expectations, based largely on the character of the missionaries they have seen and accepted as typical Americans, only to find American college students trifling away their time with matters of no importance, and social customs permitted that give the lie to all our Christian pretensions. There are always about fifteen hundred Chinese studying in America, and it is distressing to know how many of them find their spiritual foundations undermined by these unworthy examples of what a Christian community ought to be.

"It is not long since a fine Chinese friend of mine," writes one American, "who was a radiant, enthusiastic Christian when I first knew him—his very face reflecting the joy of his life—sailed back to China to become professor of history in a fine new Chinese university. He had been in this country about ten years, except for a period spent in France during the war, and he was going back a cynic, with no use for Christianity, more or less scornful of high ideals, saying that the ideals of Christianity were utterly impossible and that we ought not to offer them to people. He was almost ready to argue that Christianity had not accomplished anything good for the world and was perfectly willing to tell you that China would be better off if Christianity had never gone there."

Does there ever a Chinese enter the community in which you live? If there does, you have a responsibility toward the making of new China by giving that Chinese an object-lesson in what Christian living means. Not by preaching, but by acting, can most be done to convince these men and women who will wield large influence in the future that our Christian faith is in truth a power that will transform, even as the life of their beloved China must be transformed.

Finally, among all true Christians there should be taken such steps as will help to protect China, and all other nations, against any unrighteousness upon the part of our government and commercial interests, or upon the part of others. This means that we must cultivate the interests and outlook of world Christians. We must live on the basis already stated, that there cannot be disease of any kind—physical, industrial, or moral—in any part of the world without it being our concern. We must be as eager to see health come to men and women half a globe away as to those who live beside us on our own continent.

Much of the exploitation against which such a nation as China is now rebelling comes from the eagerness of commercial interests to reap large and easy profits. Years ago there grew up the political doctrine that a nation should support its citizens, no matter what sort of business they might engage in, outside of national boundaries. A great deal of the world's trouble has grown out of the application of that doctrine. It is time for Christian citizens to demand that, if the protection of the flag is to extend to overseas traders, those traders submit the control of their business to the government. And if this is done, it seems clear that, as world Christians, we should demand the adoption of at least three principles for the control of this overseas industry: (1) that no development of the resources of another country take place upon terms unacceptable to the people of that country; (2) that no development take place upon terms that would rob the people of that country, either temporarily or permanently, of the wealth that such resources should secure for them; (3) that no development take place upon terms that would place the value of the product above the welfare of the worker.

We must see that injustice, even when it is practised against a nation not in a position immediately to resist, leads, in the long run, to war. As world

[176]

Christians, our first concern must be for the establishment of peace among men, and peace can come only in an era that is governed by justice and truth and mutual regard.

We must recognize that the struggle that the Chinese are making to secure a better China is not an isolated struggle. It is but part of the struggle that all of us should be engaged in, to make all the lands better lands. So the setbacks of the Chinese will be one with our setbacks. So their successes will be one with ours. And we will learn, as the days pass, how to give them reinforcement in their hours of need. For the battle for a better world must be won everywhere before it can finally be won anywhere.

Let the world rejoice because China is astir. There may be discomfort in such disorders as mark the present day of transition, but there is likewise life. There is fine courage in the attempt that so many Chinese are making to produce higher levels of living, not only in the realms that we have so briefly mentioned in this book, but in other realms as well. We salute that courage. And we pledge ourselves, in the spirit of world friendliness, to help as it is possible for us to help, in order that the dreams of these brave Chinese men and women may be realized, and China's life be revolutionized, both within and without.

READING LIST

General

Beyond Shanghai. HAROLD SPEAKMAN. Abingdon Press, New York. 1922. $2.50.

Charm of the Middle Kingdom, The. J. M. MARSH. Little, Brown and Co., New York. 1922. $3.00.

China and Her Peoples. L. E. JOHNSTON. George H. Doran Co., New York. 1924. $1.50.

China: An Interpretation. JAMES W. BASHFORD. Abingdon Press, New York. 1919. $2.50.

China Awakened. M. T. Z. TYAU. The Macmillan Co., New York. 1922. $5.00.

China From Within. Impressions and Experiences. CHARLES ERNEST SCOTT. Fleming H. Revell Co., New York. 1917. $2.00.

China, Yesterday and Today. EDWARD THOMAS WILLIAMS. T. Y. Crowell Co., New York. 1923. $4.00.

Chinese Characteristics. ARTHUR HENDERSON SMITH. Fleming H. Revell Co., New York. 1900. $2.00.

Swinging Lanterns. ELIZABETH CRUMP ENDERS. D. Appleton and Co., New York. 1923. $2.50.

History and Politics

An American Diplomat in China. PAUL S. REINSCH. Doubleday, Page and Co., New York. 1922. $4.00.

China in the Family of Nations. HENRY T. HODGKIN. George H. Doran Co., New York. 1923. $2.00.

China's Story. WILLIAM ELLIOT GRIFFIS. Houghton Mifflin Co., Boston. New Edition. 1922. $1.25.

Civilization of China, The. H. A. GILES. Henry Holt Co., New York. 1911. 50 cents.

READING LIST

Fight for the Republic in China, The. B. L. Putnam Weale (B. L. Simpson). Dodd, Mead and Co., New York. 1917. $3.50.

Foreign Relations of China, The. Mingchien Joshua Bau. Fleming H. Revell Co., New York. 1921. $4.00.

Marco Polo: Travels. Translated by W. Marsden. Everyman's Library. E. P. Dutton Co., New York. 1908. 35 and 70 cents.

Outline of History. H. G. Wells. Chapter on Marco Polo. The Macmillan Co., New York. 1920. 1 vol. edition. $5.00.

Education

China in the Family of Nations. See work cited under "History and Politics." Chap. X, "The New Thought Movement."

China Today Through Chinese Eyes. Chap. II, "China's Renaissance"; Chap. III, "The Literary Revolution in China." George H. Doran Co., New York. 1923. $1.50.

Christian Education in China. Committee of Reference and Counsel. New York. 1922. $2.00.

Letters from China and Japan. John and Alice Chapman Dewey. E. P. Dutton Co., New York. 1923. $2.50.

Social and Economic Conditions

Changing Chinese, The. E. A. Ross. The Century Co., New York. 1911. $2.40.

China Awakened. See work cited under "General."

China's Place in the Sun. Stanley High. The Macmillan Co., New York. 1922. $1.75.

Farmers of Forty Centuries. F. H. King. Mrs. F. H. King. Madison, Wisconsin. 1911.

Village Life in China. Arthur H. Smith. Fleming H. Revell Co., New York. 1899. $2.50.

READING LIST

The Religions of China

China Today Through Chinese Eyes. See work cited under "Education." Chap. IV, "The Confucian God-Idea"; Chap. V, "Present Tendencies in Chinese Buddhism."

Religion of the Chinese, The. J. J. M. DeGroot. The Macmillan Co., New York. 1910. $1.25.

Religions of Mankind, The. Edmund Davison Soper. The Abingdon Press, New York. 1921. $3.00.

Three Religions of China. William Edward Soothill. George H. Doran Co., New York. 1913. $1.50.

Christianity in China

China and Modern Medicine. Harold Balme. Student Volunteer Movement, New York. 1921. Cloth, $1.25.

China's Challenge to Christianity. Lucius C. Porter. Missionary Education Movement, New York. 1924. 75 cents.

China Today Through Chinese Eyes. See work cited under "Education." Chap. VI, "The Impression of Christianity Made upon the Chinese People Through Contact with the Christian Nations of the West"; Chap. VII, "The Chinese Church."

In China Now. China's Need and the Christian Contribution. J. C. Keyte. George H. Doran Co., New York. $1.50.

Ming Kwong, the City of Morning Light. Mary Ninde Gamewell. Central Committee on the United Study of Foreign Missions, West Medford, Mass. 1924. 75 cents.

New Life Currents in China. Mary Ninde Gamewell. Missionary Education Movement, New York. 1919. Cloth, 75 cents.

Pioneering in Tibet. Albert L. Shelton. Fleming H. Revell Co., New York. 1921. $1.00.

Spread of Christianity, The. Paul Hutchinson. Chap. XXIII. Abingdon Press, New York. 1922. $1.50.

Spread of Christianity in the Modern World, The. EDWARD
CALDWELL MOORE. Chap. IX. University of Chicago
Press, Chicago. 1919. $2.00.

Art and Letters

Chinese Art Motives Interpreted. WINIFRED V. S. TREDWELL.
G. P. Putman's Sons, New York. 1915. $1.75.

History of Chinese Literature. HERBERT A. GILES. D. Appleton and Co., New York. 1921.

Lute of Jade, The. Translations by CRANMER-BYNG. E. P.
Dutton and Co., New York. 1909. 50 cents.

More Translations from the Chinese. Translated by ARTHUR
WALEY. Alfred A. Knopf, New York. 1919. $2.00.

One Hundred and Seventy Chinese Poems. An anthology of
Chinese verse from the second century B.C. up to modern
times. Translated by A. D. WALEY. Alfred A. Knopf,
New York. 1919. $2.00.

Outlines of Chinese Art. JOHN C. FERGUSON. University of
Chicago Press, Chicago. 1919. $3.00.

Studies in the Chinese Drama. K. BUSS. Four Seas Company,
Boston. 1922. $5.00.

Stories and Biographies

Bells of the Blue Pagoda. The Strange Enchantment of a
Chinese Doctor. JEAN CARTER COCHRAN. Westminster
Press, Philadelphia. 1922. $1.75.

Calvin Wilson Mateer. Forty-five Years a Missionary in
Shantung, China. DANIEL FISHER. Westminster Press,
Philadelphia. 1911. $1.50.

Chinese Fairy Book, The. FREDERICK H. and R. WILHELM
MARTENS. F. A. Stokes Co., New York. 1921. $2.50.

Chinese Nights Entertainments. Stories of Old China. BRIAN
BROWN. Brentano, New York. 1922. $2.00.

Torchbearers in China. BASIL MATHEWS. Missionary Education
Movement, New York. 1924. 75 cents.

[181]

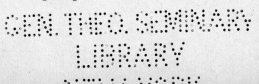

READING LIST

Foreign Magic. JEAN CARTER COCHRAN. Missionary Education Movement, New York. 1919. $1.50.

Hudson Taylor and the China Inland Mission. The Growth of a Work of God. DR. and MRS. HOWARD TAYLOR. Morgan and Scott, London. 1915.

Life of Dr. Arthur Jackson of Manchuria, The. ALFRED J. COSTAIN. Hodder and Stoughton, London. 1911.

Ministers of Mercy. JAMES H. FRANKLIN. Chap. VII, "Peter Parker." Chap. VIII, "John Kenneth Mackenzie." Missionary Education Movement, New York. 1919. 75 cents.

Nathan Sites. An Epic of the East. S. MOORE SITES. Fleming H. Revell Co., New York. 1912. $1.50.

New Lanterns in Old China. THEODORA MARSHALL INGLIS. Fleming H. Revell Co., New York. 1923. $1.25.

Noble Army, A. ETHEL DANIELS HUBBARD. Chap. VI, "Service Stars" (General Feng). Central Committee on the United Study of Foreign Missions, West Medford, Mass. 1921. 65 cents.

Notable Women of Modern China. MARGARET E. BURTON. Fleming H. Revell Co., New York. 1912. $1.50.

Robert Morrison. MARSHALL BROOMHALL. George H. Doran Co., New York. $1.50. To be published.

Servants of the King. ROBERT E. SPEER. Chap. VI, "Eleanor Chesnut"; Chap. VII, "Matthew Tyson Yates." Missionary Education Movement, New York. 1909. 75 cents.

Shelton of Tibet. MRS. A. R. SHELTON. George H. Doran Co., New York. 1923. $2.00.

Street of Precious Pearls, The. NORA WALN. The Womans Press, New York. 1921. 75 cents.

Virgil C. Hart: Missionary Statesman. E. I. HART. George H. Doran Co., New York. 1917. $1.50.

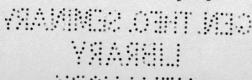